Biology
of Aging

Rockstein
& Sussman

Biology of Aging

Lifetime Series in Aging

Available now from Wadsworth:

Available now from Brooks/Cole:

Available now from Duxbury:

Forthcoming titles from Wadsworth:

Biology of Aging

Morris <u>Rockstein</u>
Marvin Sussman

Wadsworth Publishing Company
Belmont, California
A Division of Wadsworth, Inc.

Gerontology Editor: Curt Peoples
Designer: Cynthia Bassett
Scientific Illustrator: Ginny Mickelson
Cover: The new symbol of Wadsworth's *Lifetime Series in Aging* is a stylized version of the uroboros, a universal symbol for regeneration and rebirth.

Printed in the United States of America

1 2 3 4 5 6 7 8 9 10—83 82 81 80 79

Library of Congress Cataloging in Publication Data

Rockstein, Morris.
  Biology of aging.

  (Lifetime series in aging)
  Bibliography: p.
  Includes index.
    1. Aging. I. Sussman, Marvin L. II. Title.
III. Series.
QP86. R56   612.6'7   78-31912
ISBN 0-534-00687-6

Contents

To Our Children

Foreword

The appearance of this highly informative and timely volume marks the initiation of an important subseries within the Wadsworth Publishing Company's *Lifetime Series in Aging*. The scope of the subseries is to present current knowledge about the significant age-related changes affecting human beings as they move through the later decades of the life cycle. Biological, social, and cross-cultural changes highlight the initial focus of the subseries. These concerns form a vital interdisciplinary base from which students and practitioners can develop the insights and skills that can enable them to understand the needs of our growing older population.

Professors Rockstein and Sussman, in this initial subseries volume, have skillfully brought together a significant amount of material and presented it in highly readable form. They have covered the key relationships between age-related changes to the significant human biological processes: nervous system, cardiovascular system, digestive system, skin and musculoskeletal system, and the endocrine and reproductive system. They have placed these changes within a conceptual setting that underscores the emerging demographic patterns in the United States, which continue to emphasize the growing importance of the elderly in our society. Furthermore, their discussion highlights the multifaceted nature of the aging process as they discuss the biological changes within a broader context of the social and behavioral aspects of advancing years.

The volume is designed to serve the needs of upper-level undergraduates, graduate students in professional masters level programs, and professionals and practitioners who work with middle-aged and older individuals. For some it will provide sufficient information about the biological aspects of aging, while for others it is likely to provide the jumping-off point for deeper study of selected aging processes. Serving as an in-depth review and summary of our current knowledge of the biology of aging, this volume hopefully will become a standard source and reference for many years to come.

Alan D. Entine, Series Editor

Preface

In July 1965, President Lyndon B. Johnson signed Public Law 89–73. This legislation opened an era of slowly but steadily increasing concern for the development of new programs and the improvement of existing programs for providing services to the ever-growing population of older Americans. Together with its subsequent amendments, this act recognized that geriatrics, or the care and treatment of older persons, must involve a broad interdisciplinary program to be effective. It recognized that the total well-being of any individual, including the elderly, is a reflection of that individual's economic, sociological, emotional, and physical status. More and more, trained personnel are needed to deliver geriatric care, both in leadership and administrative roles and in the provision of direct services, and it is important that those who work with the elderly have an appreciation of *all* aspects of the aging process.

Biology of Aging has been designed for upper-level undergraduates, for graduate students, and for others who are training to serve the elderly in such areas as community counseling, speech and hearing, social services, continuing education, architecture, and physical education and recreation. The level and scope of the book make it appropriate for use as a primary text in introductory courses in the biology of aging or as a reference work and supplementary text for other courses in aging. It is aimed at persons with a limited biological background. Thus each chapter dealing with a human system begins with a brief survey of the normal structure of the system, amply illustrated, and of its functions; this is followed with a discussion of the details of the aging of that system. At the same time, interwoven in each chapter's discussion of "normal" and "pathological" aging are the relevant behavioral, sociological, and economic factors that affect, or are themselves affected by, the aging of that particular system. This complex interaction of all the facets of human aging is reemphasized in the final chapter, which briefly summarizes the facts of human biological aging in relation to their significance to the older person's total existence.

In addition to the specific references accompanying each chapter, a list of general references is provided at the end of the book for those interested in examining more comprehensive major works in various general or specialized areas of gerontology. The glossary is designed to clarify further for the non-biologist the technical terminology, chiefly the biomedical terms, employed and defined elsewhere in the text itself.

Biology of Aging is the product of repeated revisions of the collated results of two years of intensive research of the original literature and recent technical works on the subject of human and comparative aging. Such revisions and modifications of our original manuscript were based in part upon self-criticism and in part upon reviews by experts in the fields of biology and aging. We trust that this book will serve its intended purpose of providing a thorough, comprehensive introductory treatment of the biology of human aging.

Our sincere thanks for their helpful critical comments and suggestions are extended to Professor Allan Allenspach, Miami University, Oxford, Ohio; Dr. Sally Althoff, University of Maryland; Professor Harold Brody, State University of New York, Buffalo; Professor Delphine Eschbach, Saddleback College; Professor James R. Florini, Syracuse University; Dr. Leonard Hayflick, Children's Hospital Medical Center, Oakland, California; Professor Donald J. Kimeldorf, Oregon State University; Professor Harry Rounds, Wichita State University. To Mrs. Mercedes di Rube, we express our deep appreciation for her careful and accurate typing of the final manuscript version of this work.

Morris Rockstein, Ph. D.
Marvin L. Sussman, Ph. D.
Coral Gables, Fla.
January, 1979

About the Authors

Morris Rockstein received his Ph. D. at the University of Minnesota and, early in his career, began work in the field of biological gerontology. He has served as chairman of most major committees and as president of the American Gerontological Society and on the Council of the International Association of Gerontology. For two years, he served as Associate Director for Training at the Institute for the Study of Aging at the University of Miami. He is the author of many articles and books on the aging process in humans and other species. As professor of physiology and biophysics at the University of Miami, he currently teaches a course on the biology of human aging to undergraduates and graduates being trained for services to the elderly.

Marvin Sussman received his Ph. D. at the University of Miami. He has collaborated with Dr. Rockstein in the planning of several international symposia on aging and in the editing of several works on a number of highly technical aspects of biological gerontology.

Biology of Aging

Chapter One

Introduction

When Descartes wrote, "I think, therefore I am," he might well have added the corollary, "I think, therefore I know I shall grow old and die." Human beings have always been aware not only of their own existence but also of the fact that, with the passage of time, they must grow old and die. Such philosophical resignation to death has, for most people, lasted through the centuries. However, many fatal childhood and adult diseases (like diphtheria and smallpox) were also accepted with resignation as part of our existence until the recent development of vaccines and antibiotics conquered them. In all probability, we will never be able to avoid death, but perhaps we can learn more about prolonging life and making the aging process more agreeable.

In the last half of this century, the rapid increase in the number of people 65 and over (see Table 1.1) has caused increased interest in the physical, economic, sociological, and psychological aspects of growing old. Not only has the number of old people increased, but many people are living into their 80s and 90s; that is, the limits of human life span are expanding. Thus, more and more people are approaching the limits of longevity as we now know them.

The rapid increase in the number of older people in the United States has made our society more and more aware of the particular needs and problems of the elderly. Society in general and government in particular have become more interested in making "the golden years" more enjoyable. The White House Conferences on Aging of 1961 and 1971 reflect the recognition of those needs. Many of the recommendations of these conferences are being acted upon through the Older Americans Act of 1965 and legislation establishing programs specifically designed to help older people, such as Social Security and Medicare. Moreover, not only do we realize that our older citizens need help, but we are beginning to recognize that they can also help us. Older people possess a wealth of knowledge and experience. Programs such as SCORE (Service Core of Retired Executives) recognize the value of many

Table 1.1   Population at Age 65 and Over—United States,
1900–2000

Year	Total Population	Age 65 and Over Population	Percent
1900	75,609,000	3,099,000	4.1
1910	91,972,000	3,955,000	4.3
1920	105,700,000	5,074,000	4.8
1930	124,167,000	6,705,000	5.4
1940	132,352,000	9,000,000	6.8
1950	150,697,000	12,206,000	8.1
1960	181,076,000	16,659,000	9.2
1970	203,166,000	20,317,000	10.0
1975	215,309,000	21,816,000	10.1
1980*	227,913,000	23,703,000	10.4
1990*	252,376,000	27,509,000	10.9
2000*	272,066,000	28,839,000	10.6

*Projected.

Source: U.S. Bureau of the Census.

years of experience and call upon retired people to help in the rehabilitation of failing business ventures in fields of their own preretirement involvement. These new attitudes were voiced by the late President John F. Kennedy in his February 21, 1963, address to the Congress:

> On the basis of his study of the world's great civilizations, the historian Toynbee concluded that a society's quality and durability can best be measured "by the respect and care given to its elderly citizens." Never before in history have we had so many "senior citizens". . . . This increase in the lifespan and in the number of our senior citizens presents this Nation with increased opportunities: the opportunity to draw upon their skill and sagacity and the opportunity to provide the respect and recognition they have earned. It is not enough for a great nation merely to have added new years to life—our objective must also be to add life to those years.

This statement also reflects the basic aim of the research gerontologist, whose concern is not so much increasing the length of life, but improving the quality of life into the last years of each person's existence—that is, making "living longer better." The steady increase in the number of old and very old people has caused an increase in the number of acute and chronic health care facilities and a large demand for professionals and paraprofessionals (such as geriatric physicians, nurses, psychologists, social workers, etc.) to care for our senior citizens. However, the demand for specialists trained in **gerontology** and **geriatrics** has increased more rapidly than the supply. Courses dealing with the problems of the aged were, until recently, limited to upper graduate levels. However, the increased interest in aging and the greater demand for people trained in this area has moved the study of aging to the college and beginning graduate levels of instruction.

This book is designed for a course in the biology of aging, emphasizing human aging. It has been divided into fifteen chapters. Several brief introductory chapters cover the subject of biology of aging in general to serve as background for the more comprehensive review of the biology of human aging presented in subsequent chapters. The chapters that follow cover the changes, as one ages, in both structure and function in those organs of the human body for which such information is reasonably well-documented. Diseases known to be especially prevalent with advancing age are discussed briefly, where appropriate. The net effect of "normal biological" and "pathological" aging of the various organ systems on the capacity of the individual to cope with such changes with advancing age is also covered in each case. Two chapters cover special problems of the elderly, i.e., nutrition and sexual function. The book concludes with an overview chapter of the biology of aging as part of the *total* process of human aging (that is, the economic, sociological, and behavioral facets of the human aging process). Following are brief summaries of the material covered in each chapter.

1. Introduction.

2. The Study of the Biology of Aging.   In this chapter, the major concepts in the biology of aging are defined and discussed. More specifically these include the complexity of human aging, social consequences of aging, universal manifestations of aging, and humans versus animals in the study of aging.

3. Longevity.   This chapter begins with an explanation of the concept of longevity. The **demography** of the United States is covered, with emphasis on those factors contributing to the longevity of individuals in our society. The chapter also deals with the role of intrinsic and extrinsic determinants of longevity.

4. Theories of Aging.   Major theories of aging are defined and discussed with major emphasis on their possible involvement in human aging.

5. The Nervous System.   A general overview of the aging of the nervous system is presented in this chapter. Included are the known anatomical and functional changes in the older individual. These changes are discussed with specific reference to changes in IQ and memory, to organic brain syndrome, etc., all in relation to behavioral changes in the older person.

A review of the major changes in the various senses in relation to the health and safety of the older individual, is also included.

6. The Cardiovascular System.   This chapter examines the biological and pathological aging of this important system. It includes a consideration of arteriosclerosis and atherosclerosis as diseases especially prevalent in the older individual (and their relationship to heart attacks and strokes).

7. The Respiratory System.   Age-related changes in the physiological capacities of the lungs are covered. Diseases like emphysema and lung cancer are discussed in relation to likely, underlying contributory, environmental factors.

8. The Gastrointestinal System.   Age-related changes in the digestive tract and pathological states like cancer are covered in this chapter.

9. The Urinary System.   Aging in the structure and function of the kidney are reviewed.

10. Nutrition.   Known dietary and nutritional needs of the elderly are discussed in relation to a lifelong nutrition program. Vitamins and minerals and the use of specific foods are also discussed with relation to aging.

11. The Skin, Bone, and Muscle.   The physiology and pathology of the aging skin and hair are reviewed briefly. Age-related changes in bone tissue and their effects on the human skeleton are discussed. Anatomical and functional changes in muscle are also reviewed.

12. The Endocrine System.   This chapter surveys known changes in the endocrine system and the hormones produced with advancing age.

13. The Reproductive System.   This chapter discusses the changes which occur in the male and female reproductive systems. The psychological and sociological implications of aging reproductive and sexual functions are discussed.

14. Sexual Competency and Aging.   The physiological and behavioral changes in the sexuality of the elderly are dealt with. Emphasis is placed not only on their biological bases, but also upon the sociobehavioral factors involved.

15. Human Aging: A Multifaceted Phenomenon.   The combined effects of the physiological and pathological changes in the elderly are discussed in relation to social, psychological, and economic elements involved in the aging process.

References

Kennedy, J. F. 1963. Elderly citizens of our nation. 88th Congress. First Session. House Document 72, Feb. 21, pp. 1–16.

Note: A list of General References is given on pages 191–192.

Chapter Two

The Study of the Biology of Aging

The Complexity of Human Aging

Throughout this book, the one underlying principle emphasized is that human **aging** is a complex process that cannot be discussed in purely biological terms. Human aging must be considered as the *sum* of biological, social, economic, and psychological changes that occur with advancing age. These internal and external changes are not only interactive but often interdependent. Together they produce the complex process of aging in the human being.

Biological aging refers, of course, to the time-related changes in the anatomy and physiology of the individual. The effects of changes in financial status that alter the life style of the older person can be referred to as *economic aging*. Additionally, lifelong economic factors ranging from poor housing, diet, and health and dental care on the poverty level to rich foods and a lack of exercise due to the overuse of labor-saving devices among the middle class and the wealthy all contribute, in one way or another, to the normal and pathological course of aging. Age-related changes in the individual's behavioral adaptive capacities are involved in *psychological aging*. *Social aging* has to do with acquired social habits, social status, and the individual's changing social roles with the passage of time. Especially important are the changes in the role of the older person in the family and in the community, which influence both social and psychological aging. In this chapter and throughout this book, we will see how these various biological, economic, social, and psychological dimensions interact in the process of human aging.

Biological Aging

As with any new subject, we must define the major concepts on which we will depend to build our understanding of the biology of aging.

What is *aging,* and how does it differ from **senescence?** Is an infant or a young child aging? In order to answer these and related questions, we will first review the biological stages of life.

The Biological Stages of Life

Biologists think of life in three distinct stages: embryological development, growth and **maturation,** and senescence. *Embryological development* begins at the moment the sperm fertilizes the egg and lasts until the organism is born. *Growth* and *maturation* are the continued development of the organism from birth through adulthood, into the prime of life. During *senescence,* the final stage, the body's ability to reverse the degenerative changes in structure and function (such as the speed of wound healing or recovery from illness) becomes less effective and, ultimately, fails. These three stages, taken together, are known as the life span of the organism and form a continuum of time-directed changes in the organism's anatomy and physiology. *Aging,* which actually begins at fertilization, can be defined as the sum of all the changes that normally occur in an organism with the passage of time. Senescence, or growing old, is but the last stage of the lifelong process of aging.

Aging

When speaking of age changes in the body of any organism, there are two important principles to remember: namely, (1) in any one organism, *all* organs do not age at the same rate, and (2) any one **organ** (e.g., the heart, stomach, or brain) does not necessarily age at the same rate in different individuals of the same species. These principles are, in fact, most likely to apply to human beings because we are the single most heterogeneous species on earth in our genetic make-up.

Human aging as a total process begins at conception, accelerates, and becomes most noticeable in late middle age (in the fifth and sixth decades of life) when the outward signs of aging—graying hair, wrinkling skin, diminishing muscle strength—become apparent. The "old" individual is further characterized by bent posture, slower movement, a number of sensory deficits (in eyesight and hearing especially), typical personality changes (such as forgetfulness or belligerence), and a greater incidence of certain **chronic diseases** (Table 2.1).[1] However, as already noted, aging does not begin *sud-*

---

[1]Health care statistics for the aged dramatically illustrate the increasing incidence of chronic disease in people aged 65 and over. This age group currently represents about 10 percent of the population, but they account for 14.5 percent of persons hospitalized in the United States. Their average length of stay in the hospital is twice as great as for persons in the 45 to 64 age group (13.8 days versus 6.5 days).

A major consideration for the retired person over 65 is the cost of health care. In 1970, for example, the elderly spent more than three times as much on health care as those persons

Table 2.1   Percent Incidence of Major Chronic Diseases—
United States, 1960–1970

Condition	All Ages	Under 45	45–64	64 and Over
Heart Conditions	15.5	6.3	19.0	20.5
Arthritis and Rheumatism	14.1	4.4	15.7	21.2
Visual Impairment	4.8	3.6	3.8	7.0
Noncardiac-involved hypertension	4.6	1.8	5.2	6.4
Mental and nervous conditions	4.4	5.3	5.0	3.0

Source: National Health Survey. All data refer to persons with limitation in activity.

denly at middle age; it represents a slow, progressive, cumulative series of changes throughout our entire lives. The signs of biological aging are only part of the total series of aging changes, but they are generally observed earlier than the less obvious decrements in psychological and social capacities and functions.

The course of aging varies from individual to individual depending on various genetic, social, psychological, and economic factors. Thus, as we mentioned earlier, biological aging does not proceed at the same rate in different individuals in regard either to individual organs or to the total person. Accordingly, using chronological age (whether age 65, 70, or even 80) as a magic dividing line between "old" and "not-old" is, at best, an economic convenience but certainly not a valid biological criterion. A football player, for example, is considered "old" at 40, but a concert pianist of the same age may be at the height of his or her career and continue virtuoso performances for many decades after that. Alex Comfort (1976) cites many notable figures in the fields of politics, medicine, and the arts who made some of their most important contributions after age 65, the age at which most people are forced to retire. Thus, chronological age must not be considered the *only* criterion for compulsory retirement. Other factors, such as biological age as an index of *physical ability* to perform a particular role and a person's social and psychological age, must be considered together in order to assess the need for a person to retire.

Senescence

Senescence, the final biological stage in any organism's life, is a period during which the degenerative processes that cause an organism to

---

under 65 years old ($791 per capita versus $226 per capita). In actual total dollars paid, $10,619,100,000 came from public funds, including $6.8 billion from Medicare and $2.5 billion from Medicaid. In 1970, then, federal funds paid 87 percent of the bill for delivery of medical care to only 10 percent of the population.

break down are not balanced by the repair mechanisms. The organism's ability to adapt and survive therefore diminishes during this period. Familiar examples of this process are stray dogs and cats who are often able to survive in the streets for many years. As they grow older, however, their reflexes slow, increasing their chances of being struck by a car, and their ability to survive injuries diminishes. Senescence in humans refers to that portion of the aging process that society calls "growing old." It is during this final stage of aging that the most rapid rate of decline takes place. No one, however, really dies from old age. Usually, there is a specific cause of death, such as a disease or organ failure. The puristic gerontologist would say that the real cause of death in truly *normal* aging (involving *physiological* rather than *pathological* processes) is the failure of a *specific* organ or organs and would eliminate any reference to disease. For example, most deaths can be attributed to four major causes; these are heart and circulatory failure, brain failure, respiratory failure, and kidney failure. However, as we shall see below, the likelihood of contracting and succumbing to most diseases increases logarithmically as one grows older (Table 2.1). Moreover, even when older people survive a specific disease, they are left in a weakened state and may find it more difficult to endure another stressful situation.

Traumatic experiences may likewise weaken an individual. The death of a spouse, forced retirement, and other psychological and social realities associated with advancing age (such as a fear of illness or institutionalization) may result in an older person's neglect of his or her diet, health care, and general welfare. These and many other factors may accelerate the processes of senescence.

Social Consequences of Aging

In our society, retirement is usually considered to be synonomous with a specific chronological age. Regardless of whether a person has been employed in a professional, managerial, blue collar, or service position, the retiree gives up a defined socioeconomic position in society in general and in the family as well. The retirement income may be a fraction of what it had been during working years. The retiree may be forced to sell the longtime family residence and move to a small apartment either for financial reasons or because physical disabilities make maintenance of a large dwelling impossible. Luxuries in life style, likewise, must be reduced or eliminated. A person such as a single widowed grandparent, once the center of attention as head of the family, experiences a diminished role when obliged to live in the home of his or her child. Thus, both family position and income are diminished with loss of job status or a reduction in physical and mental capacities.

Outside of the family environment, limitations in income make it difficult if not impossible for the older person to keep up with changing fashions of dress and hair style. This makes the older person look and feel out-of-date. Such people may be forced to limit their social activities in order to keep within the small, static income that has an ever-diminishing purchasing power. Financial expeditures on subscriptions to concert and opera series, membership dues at social clubs, or even simple activities like attending a movie become more difficult and often impossible. Finally, the cost of both automobile insurance and maintenance and an increasing physical debility tend to limit the older person's mobility and therefore his social activities as well.

These psychological, social, and economic limitations on retired people are further aggravated by society's negative **stereotypes** of the elderly. "Putting the elderly to pasture" through compulsory retirement at a certain age and negative attitudes toward age-related changes in anatomy and physiology reduce the older persons' sense of self-worth and thus their ability and desire to continue in both career and social roles they had filled earlier in life. Such a situation often produces major behavioral and personality changes in the form of resentment, great self-isolation, and even complete withdrawal from all social activities. Finally, the increased incidence in the number and severity of various diseases and a general reduction in the capacity to deal with stress also contribute adversely to the attitudes and norms of the older individual.

Universal Manifestations of Aging

As will be emphasized throughout this book, aging is a universal phenomenon in all animals. Age-related anatomical and physiological changes may be observed in vertebrates and invertebrates if one is trained to recognize them. However, it is extremely difficult to find animals in the wild in which aging changes may be observed because these animals seldom survive to old age. Animals in their natural environment often succumb to disease, natural predators, or accident long before the changes of senescence can occur. For the same reason that longevity data are available for such animals chiefly from protected environments, observation of structural changes that indicate advanced old age may also be best observed under protected conditions, whether in zoos, aquariums, or laboratories.

Anatomical Aspects

Hair. (The graying and thinning of hair with age are changes which are not unique to human beings. Several domesticated animals, such as horses, dogs, and sheep, also develop gray hair in old age. Surprisingly, insects such as bees lose most of their fine body hairs as they grow older.

Teeth.   An old person who has not received adequate, lifelong dental care usually has worn, decaying, broken, or missing teeth. Such dental conditions are also very commonly observed in old animals, like mice, deer, elephants, horses, dogs, cats, and camels. In fact, one of the best ways to estimate an animal's age is to examine its teeth.

Body Weight.   Mammals generally tend to gain weight until they reach maturity. Unfortunately, as most of us know all too well, weight gain in human beings continues well beyond adolescence. However, during their final years of life, old people tend to undergo a loss of weight. Weight loss also occurs in old age in animals. White mice, for example, gain weight steadily during the first year of life, after which their weight gradually declines through old age.

Nervous System.   A common occurrence in the nervous systems of many different species of animals (e.g., rats, mice, insects, and humans) is the general decline in the number of nerve cells with advancing age.

Muscle Mass.   **Skeletal muscle** tissue undergoes an age-related decrease in mass due to a reduction in the number or volume of *muscle fibers* (the cells which make up muscle) or both. Skeletal muscle is not capable of replacing fibers that have been destroyed by environmental stresses. The decrease in muscle tissue mass is readily observable in people of advanced old age, as evidenced by limp, hanging muscles and weakened muscle strength. Similar changes have been observed in several strains of rats.

Aging Pigments.   The accumulation of aging pigment granules as an animal gets older (particularly in cardiac muscle cells and nerve cells) is a phenomenon which has been widely demonstrated in many species. These pigments are generally termed **lipofuscin,** although their composition may vary from one species to another. In humans, aging pigments have been found to accumulate in many different tissues. (These will be discussed in later chapters in relation to the specific organ systems in which they are found.) Most mammals and many invertebrates (e.g., protozoa and insects) exhibit such increasing pigment deposition with advancing age.

Physiological Manifestations

Motor Activity.   A familiar stereotype of an elderly person involves slowness of movement with diminished muscle strength. An age-related decrease in motor activity occurs in almost all animal species, most notably humans, dogs, rats, mice, bees, and flies. In fact, since the flight muscle of insects has both structural and functional features which are analogous to higher vertebrate skeletal muscle (including that of human beings), it has been used as a convenient model system for the study of the aging of muscle in humans.

Reproductive Senescence.   A decline in reproductive activity and fertility occurs in all animals at advanced ages. Although only the human female undergoes menopause (sometime during the fifth decade of life), other animals do undergo reproductive senescence with advancing age. In mice, rats, dogs, and hamsters, fewer offspring per litter are produced, and there is a progressively longer interval between litters. Similarly, egg production in domestic fowl and the number of viable offspring produced by some live-bearing fish also decrease with advancing maternal age.

Adaptability to Stress.   Perhaps the most universal aging phenomenon is the progressively decreasing ability to adapt to environmental stresses, which leads to a time-dependent increase in the mortality rate. This has been demonstrated in a number of experiments performed using laboratory animals, such as mice and rats.

Humans Versus Animals in the Study of Aging

The human being, one of the longest-lived mammals, is, unfortunately, a poor model for the scientific study of aging. Since the life span of the scientist studying human aging is similar to that of his subjects, it is nearly impossible to make a longitudinal study of aging on the same subject or group of subjects from birth to death. To collect such data, the scientist would have to outlive the subjects, which is virtually impossible considering the age at which most scientists begin their careers. This problem has been eliminated in part by the use of *cross-sectional studies* in which average (hopefully normal) men and women from each of a number of different age groups are studied for specific physical and physiological changes.

There are several advantages to using animals as models in any scientific research, including the study of aging. In fact, the use of suitable animals has a solid rationale in terms of the universality of the aging process. Furthermore, it is highly desirable that the genetic make-up of the experimental animal under investigation be fairly uniform. The use of completely pure genetic strains is most desirable, if available. Humans, however, are probably the single most hybridized species of animal on earth. The genetic make-up of every person represents hundreds of generations of cross breeding of different cultures and races. For this reason, except in the case of identical twins, every human being has a pattern of genes vastly different from virtually anyone else on earth, including one's parents, brothers, and sisters. On the other hand, the longterm inbreeding of specific strains of laboratory animals has made possible the establishment of colonies of animals with known characteristics, which are frequently genetically pure for a particular trait (see p. 30). Experimental genetic inbreeding in humans (amounting to incest) is, of course, impossible.

Environmental considerations are equally important. The human environment is highly varied and constantly changing. Indeed, for two persons living in the same neighborhood or even in the same apartment building, any number of living conditions may be entirely dissimilar. Common variables include the ambient (room) temperature, the length of the work day, exposure to stress, diet, and health maintenance habits. On the contrary, in animal studies, it is possible to maintain carefully controlled environmental conditions, which yield highly reproducible results. If one were to perform such studies on humans, only longterm confinement could produce even a vestige of such controlled environmental conditions. Where such unusual conditions do exist—in a prison or a longterm care facility such as a nursing home—they can hardly be considered favorable for scientific studies.

There are obvious limitations on the type and scope of experiments which can be carried out on human beings. People will normally not submit to procedures which they find objectionable. Moreover, government regulations very strictly control the kind of experiments which can be carried out on human subjects. One recently publicized case emphasizes the necessity of these restrictions. A study was made involving prison inmates during the 1950s to determine the end-stage effects of **syphilis.** Most of the subjects were treated for their disease, but a control group of subjects was not treated. The families of the inmates who had died or become permanently disfigured because of the lack of treatment were later awarded millions of dollars in damages.

There are also fairly stringent regulations insuring the humane treatment of animals in experimental studies. Nevertheless, there is obviously a much wider latitude in the range and types of experiments that can be performed on animals than on human subjects. Before a vaccine, therapeutic drug, or food additive is made available for human use, it is clearly mandatory to test its use in lower animals for possible injurious side effects. For similar reasons, studies involving potentially dangerous environmental factors, such as ionizing radiation, have been made primarily in rodents and insects. However, data on radiation for humans have been available both from industrial radiation accidents and from studies of the survivors of the atom bomb in Hiroshima and Nagasaki.

Unfortunately, human studies involve much longer periods than animal studies, so that the subjects may lose interest or move away from the project and therefore be lost to the study. Likewise, many people do not follow directions properly unless closely supervised. Thus, despite all precautions, consistently valid experiments on humans are difficult to run. Obviously, all of these problems are minimized in animal experiments where controlled experimental conditions can be maintained.

Animal Models

We have seen why the human being is a poor model for research on aging and why lower animals are more useful models. In determining which animals are the most useful for study, several attributes must be considered, as we have indicated above. First of all, the experimental animal should have a *short life span* relative to that of their human investigators (see Table 2.2). They should be *small in size* so that they can be maintained in large numbers in a relatively limited amount of space. They should be available in long-inbred or preferably *genetically pure strains.* Finally, the animal model employed should exhibit the same *aging characteristics* that are found in humans. A survey of gerontological literature reveals that most of the animals used successfully in past and current research in aging do indeed meet these criteria.

Although *insect* species seem highly unlikely experimental animals for the study of aging, they actually meet, better than most other animals, all of the above-mentioned criteria. Indeed, most of the important early studies in modern genetics were made on the fruit fly, *Drosophila.* Most importantly, insects possess functional and structural features (including *cell size*) analogous to mammals, including humans. Furthermore, the complex biochemical processes involved in cellular **metabolism** in insects are virtually identical with those in humans and other mammals.

Inbred and genetically pure strains of laboratory *rodents,* such as Wistar and Fischer rats and many strains of mice, have relatively short life spans (about two years) and are easily maintained in sizeable numbers in relatively little space. Many aging studies have been performed on these animals, including the classical investigations of the role of nutrition in aging (see Chapter 10).

Compared to rodents and insects, *dogs* have a relatively long average life span: 10 years or more. However, dogs suffer from many diseases also common in older people, such as cataracts, loss of sight and hearing, bone deterioration, prostate dysfunction, and muscle weakness. Thus, although longitudinal aging studies with dogs require relatively long periods of time, because of the similarity of canine diseases in old age to those occurring in humans, such longterm studies can be extremely valuable.

Table 2.2   Longevity Values for Several Species of Mammals

		Life Span	
Common Name	Scientific Name	Mean (yr.)	Maximum (yr.)
Primates			
Human	*Homo sapiens*	70.8	115.0
Chimpanzee	*Pan troglodytes*	17.5	44.5
Artiodactyla			
Domestic cattle	*Bos taurus*	23.0	30.0
Swine	*Sus scrofa*	16.0	27.0
Sheep	*Ovis aries*	12.0	20.0
Goat	*Capra hircus*	9.0	18.0
Perissodactyla			
Horse	*Equus caballus*	25.0	62.0
Proboscidea			
Elephant, Indian	*Elephas maximus*	40.0	70.0
Carnivora			
Cat	*Felis catus*	15.0	28.0
Domestic dog	*Canis familiaris*	15.0	34.0
Rodentia			
Gray squirrel	*Sciurus carolinensis*	9.0	15.0
Mouse	*Mus musculus*	1.5	3.5
House rat	*Rattus rattus*	2.5	4.7
European rabbit	*Oryctolagus cuniculus*	5.5	13.0
Guinea pig	*Cavia porcellus*	2.0	7.5
Golden hamster	*Mesocricetus auratus*	2.0	4.0

Although *swine* are even longer lived than dogs (over 15 years), they have proven particularly useful in studies of **atherosclerosis** and obesity, conditions which they share with man, particularly as they age.

Thus, we have seen that animal models are extremely important in any basic research program but are especially important in the study of such a universally distributed phenomenon as aging. Comparative studies involving animals other than humans serve not only to define the facts of aging, but particularly to focus on the mechanisms underlying the aging process. The basic biological scientist, using the results of such studies on animal models, may eventually be able to use this knowledge to our benefit to make "living longer better."

References

Dublin, L. I., A. J. Lotka, and M. Spiegelman. 1949. Length of life. The Ronald Press, New York. 379 pp.

Rockstein, M. 1974. The old frontier. Medical Dimensions, Nov.: 35–42.

The Concept of Longevity

      Mean Longevity
      Maximum Longevity

Demography: The Statistical Aspects of Longevity

      Life Expectancy
      Sex Ratios in the Aged
      Major Causes of Death

Intrinsic Determinants: The Genetic Basis for Longevity

      Genealogical Studies
      Life Insurance Statistics
      Studies of Twins
      Species-Specific Longevity
      Sex Differences and Longevity
      Experimental Inbreeding of Longevity

Extrinsic Determinants: Environmental Influences on Longevity

      Parental Age
      Radiation
      Disease
      Marital Status

References

Chapter Three

Longevity

The length of time that any organism lives depends on a number of factors. The determinants of longevity include both the genetic make-up of the organism, the *intrinsic* factors, and those arising from the environment, the *extrinsic* factors. Intrinsic factors are the basic determinants of the maximum possible longevity of an organism. On the other hand, the extrinsic factors, superimposed upon the basic, genetically predicted life span, can modify that expression so as to shorten life span, often drastically.

Senescence is, as we have previously stated, the final stage in a series of events known as the life span of the individual. In order to have an idea of the total time course of the aging process, gerontologists must first determine the longevity of the organism.

The Concept of Longevity

We can examine aging within any population as either (1) the aging of any one individual or of the *average* individual within the group or (2) the aging of the population as a whole. In either case, we must first have a good idea of the total span of time involved, that is, of the length of life or *longevity*[1] of the organism. Longevity, as a comparative term, defines the *duration* of life of an individual member of a particular species or population. For such a species or population, there are two measurements of longevity: *mean longevity* and *maximum longevity.*

Mean Longevity

The mean or average longevity of a population is calculated by dividing the total of the ages at death of all the members of a population by the

---

[1] A common fallacy among gerontologists and the general population alike is that aging and longevity are synonymous. However, *aging* refers to the sum of change within the individual over time, whereas *longevity* refers simply to the length of life.

number of individuals in that population. For example, if we select a litter of five kittens as our population and follow them throughout life, we can calculate their mean longevity. Let us assume that one dies at 1 year of age, two die at 4 years, one at 6 years, and one at 13 years. Thus, this five-member population lived a total of 28 (1 + 4 + 4 + 6 + 13) years, and the mean or average longevity for this group is 5.6 years (28 years divided by 5, the size of the population). The larger the population size studied, the more statistically valid will be the calculated mean longevity. For humans, **life expectancy** is the same as mean longevity for a given population during a specific period of time (see Table 3.1). It is based on the ages at death of all members of a particular population (whether for a city or worldwide) for a given census period (usually 10 years).

For humans, mean longevity values have continuously increased through the centuries. Although the *maximum* human life span has not expanded, more individuals now live to older ages due to advances in medical science, especially in immunology and antibiotic therapy. For example, increases in mean longevity values since the beginning of this century have been brought about in part by a significant reduction in infant mortality through the elimination of many childhood diseases, such as smallpox, diphtheria, and polio.

Statistics on mean longevity taken over a given period of time (usually one or ten years) may be influenced by certain migration patterns of the population. This is more significant in recent years due to the increased mobility of the population made possible by modern transportation. The movement of older persons into states like Florida and California, for example, would tend to negate the significance of distribution of mean longevity by state.

Maximum Longevity

In contrast to mean longevity, *maximum longevity* does not involve a statistical calculation, since it is simply the record of the age at death of the longest-lived members of a population. It is like a fact in a "believe-it-or-

Table 3.1   Human Life Expectancy in the United States

	Year							
	1776	*1900*	*1920*	*1940*	*1950*	*1960*	*1970*	*1975*
Life Expectancy at birth (years)	35	49	59	64	68	70	70	72

Source: U.S. Bureau of the Census.

not'' book or, to the sports aficionado, a record such as *the most home runs,* or *the lowest earned run average.*

There have been valid, authenticated reports of maximum longevity values for humans somewhere between 110 and 120 years of age. Although we know that humans represent the longest-lived species of mammals, collection of accurate longevity data for human populations on a global basis is difficult and subject to many errors in sampling. The records for the longest-lived humans, in fact, all come from primitive areas, such as the rural villages of Russia, America, and Tibet, where births, if noted at all, were frequently recorded in the family Bible along with deaths and marriages. Families often used the names of children who had died in infancy for later offspring without correcting the original birth records. A further complication is that many people, when asked their ages, tend to understate or overstate them, depending on the situation. An old person, for example, might exaggerate his or her age either for attention or for the reverence which extreme old age seems to command.[2]

Mean and maximum longevity are values concerning individuals. Mean longevity is the life expectancy of the average individual, and maximum longevity is actually the longest life span known and recorded for a given population. However, in order to plan for the future needs of a society due to changes in the population (such as increases in the number of elderly people, migration patterns, etc.), it is not enough to study the vital statistics for individuals. It is also necessary to study the **demography** of the population in question.

Demography: The Statistical Aspects of Longevity

Demography is the study of the distribution of changes and trends in births, marriages, diseases, and deaths in a given population. Statistical aging trends in a population result from the interaction of the three major factors of birth, migration, and number of deaths at different ages. An increase or decrease in births will add to or decrease the size of the elderly population 65 years later. Migration will add either young or old individuals to the population, altering the composition of the group in question. Changes in mortality will either reduce the size of the population which will eventually become old (with increased mortality) or (with decreased mortality) increase the size of

[2]For a critical review of the facts on humans approaching longevities of over 150 years of age, see the reports by Meyers (1966) and Medvedev (1974) which help to resolve the apparent contradictions between the reported age and the *true* maximum life spans of humans of 110 to 120 years of age.

this group. A demographer may describe a population as aging either by its *median age* or by the *number* of old people in it.

Life Expectancy

Unlike maximum longevity, *average longevity* (life expectancy at birth) has continued to increase since the beginning of the century (Table 3.1). For example, an individual born in 1900 into the United States population was, on the day of birth, expected to live about 49 years. By 1950, this life expectancy had increased to about 69 years. From 1950 to 1970, however, life expectancy at birth increased only slightly, representing, perhaps, a temporary leveling off in the number of people saved through the then available medical care. In 1975, life expectancy for *all* persons at birth in the United States rose even further to 72 years. Differentiated by sex, life expectancy was 68.2 years for men and 75.9 years for women. (The figures are slightly higher for white males and white females.) Thus the population of the United States is sometimes described as steadily "getting older," because the proportion of people 65 and over is continuously increasing. This existing trend in aging statistics of a growing population 65 years of age in the United States is due for the most part to (1) a general *rise* in the number of births at the turn of the century, (2) heavy immigration from Europe just before and after World War I, and (3) declining mortality rates in all age groups as a result of improved medical care, including early detection and treatment of heart disease and cancer.

But just how rapidly is the size of our elderly population increasing? As shown in Table 1.1, in the census of 1900, about 3.1 million Americans were over the age of 65. In 1920, almost 5.1 million Americans had reached this age, and by 1940, the number had reached 9 million. Only 30 years later, in 1970, 20.3 million people were "senior citizens." Over the last 80 years, the number of older citizens in the United States has been increasing at a rate of 300,000 to 400,000 people per year. By the beginning of the twenty-first century, if current trends continue, 29 million people (over 10 percent of the population) will face the concomitants of old age.

In contrast to the group born in 1900, during the Depression years (1929–1935) there was a significant *decrease* in the birth rate. Unless offset by migration or decreased mortality rates, this should result in a *decrease* in the percentage of elderly people 65 years later, i.e., in the 1994 to 2000 population census (see Table 1.1). On the other hand, the "baby boom" following World War II (during the years 1945–1957) should result in a marked *increase* in the number and percentage of older Americans in 2012 to 2022, whereas the reduced birth rates of the 1970s could, conversely, mean a decrease in the proportion of elderly people after the 2030 census.

Sex Ratios in the Aged

Forty years ago, the population of the United States had equal numbers of women and men age 65 and over. As Table 3.2 shows, since that time this ratio has increasingly favored females, until today, the elderly population consists of 100 women for every 72 men (or 138 women to every 100 men). If current trends continue, this disparity will continue to increase. For example, in 1980 the sex ratio is expected to reach 145:100 and by 1990, 148:100. However, females do not outnumber males throughout all age groups of the population. In the newborn to 5-year-old group, boys slightly outnumber girls. The reversal of the sexual majority from birth to old age is due to sex differences in mortality rates. In addition to the possible genetic differences favoring females, males have a higher mortality rate because of higher incidences of fatal illnesses earlier in life and, later, death from the casualties of war, violence, and serious accidents. However, the incidence by sex of chronic, debilitating diseases is somewhat unexpected (Table 3.3), since the lower mortality rate of women should logically be associated with a lower incidence of these diseases. Thus, with the exception of heart conditions and visual impairments, all of the disorders listed were more common in women than in men. Especially notable was the incidence in women of **arthritis** and rheumatism and high blood pressure (**hypertension**) not related to heart conditions. Visual impairments showed equal distribution in both sexes.

Table 3.2   Sex Ratios of Persons Age 65 and Over—
United States, 1920–1990

	Year						
	1920	*1930*	*1950*	*1960*	*1970*	*1980**	*1990**
Female:male	98.5:100	100:100	108:100	121:100	138:100	145:100	148:100

*Projected.
Source: U.S. Bureau of the Census.

Table 3.3   Incidence of Chronic Diseases in Persons Age 65
and Over—United States, 1969–1970

Condition	Male	Female
Heart Conditions	21.8%	19.3%
Arthritis and Rheumatism	14.4%	27.1%
Visual Impairments	7.0%	7.0%
Noncardiac-involved hypertension	4.0%	8.5%
Mental and nervous conditions	2.6%	3.4%

Source: National Health Survey.

Major Causes of Death

As explained earlier, life expectancy at birth is a value determined by the number of deaths at all ages in a population. People saved from death from a particular cause must eventually die from another one (heart disease, cancer, lung diseases, etc.). For example, an infant surviving an attack of a serious disease may, 50 years later, succumb to cancer. However, the greater the number of such successfully survived incidents, the greater the (paradoxical) likelihood of *living longer* as we grow older. Thus, as death rates at different ages decline, people can expect to live longer. Table 3.4 shows that, whereas at birth a male child has a life expectancy of 67 years, at age 65 a man's life expectancy has increased to 78 years (11 years more). Similarly, a female child with a life expectancy of 74.6 years at birth, at age 65 has a life expectancy of 81.8 years (17 years more). Such increases in life expectancy have come from great reduction of infant mortality and an only moderate improvement in mortality rates of those aged 50 and over. For example, as mentioned earlier, smallpox, diphtheria, and polio, major killers of infants and young children, have been almost completely eliminated through the development of vaccines. The main causes of death in adults, however, (**atherosclerosis,** heart disease, **stroke,** and cancer) still remain the major causes of death.

Nevertheless, the elimination of *all* human diseases and *all* fatalities from war and accidents would not confer anything close to immortality. If, for

Table 3.4   Expectation of Life at Various Ages by Sex —
United States, 1969–1971

| Age (years) | Expectation of Life in Years | | |
	Male	Female	Total Persons
Birth	67.0	74.6	70.7
10	59.0	66.3	62.6
20	49.5	56.6	53.0
30	40.5	47.0	43.7
40	31.5	37.6	34.5
50	23.1	28.8	25.9
60	16.0	20.6	18.3
65	13.0	16.8	15.0
70	10.4	13.4	12.0
75	8.1	10.3	9.3
80	6.3	7.7	7.1
85	4.7	5.6	5.3

Source: National Center for Health Statistics, U.S. Public Health Service.

example, all human cancers were cured, life expectancy for the entire population would be expected to increase by only about 2 years. If all cardiovascular
diseases were eliminated, we could anticipate an additional 17 more years of
life expectancy. Prevention of all accidents (including those caused by motor
vehicles) would increase life expectancy only about 1.2 years, and the
miraculous disappearance of **pneumonia,** influenza, infectious diseases,
diabetes, and **tuberculosis** might add, at best, only one more year of life.
Eradication, then of *all* of the major causes of death (affecting adults primarily) could increase life expectancy at birth another 20 years, that is, from the
current figure of 70 to 90 years of age.

Intrinsic Determinants: The Genetic Basis For Longevity

The single most important part of the basic "machinery" of any
organism is its genetic program. This program is contained in the **genes,**
themselves borne by the **chromosomes,** which in turn are found within the
nucleus of each cell of every organism. In the cells of every individual of
every species of plants or animals, there is a characteristic encoded sequence
of genes which are inherited from their parents. It is these coded sequences of
genes which determine the characteristics of the offspring. Thus, they are
responsible for all features of the individual, including its size, shape, and
form or the nature and functioning of each cell in each of the body's component organs. When people describe a child as having its mother's eyes or its
father's nose, it is understood that they are talking about inherited characteristics. Essentially, such resemblance between child and parents reflects the
coded information in the genes inherited from one's ancestors. Likewise, the
great variability in physical characteristics from species to species, as well as
among members within the same species, is due to variations in the patterns of
genes which each has inherited.

The program provided by the **genetic code** is essentially nothing
more than a list of instructions for the various stages of our lives. Thus, for
example, the genetic code for human beings dictates that the embryo or fetus
takes approximately nine months to develop within the womb. Similarly,
sexual maturation occurs at about 12 to 14 years of age, and maturity, given a
relatively steady state of health, lasts for an average of 40 years thereafter. In
the same way that the genetic program dictates the time of onset of these
important stages in life, it also codes for the potential *maximum* life span to
which each individual can expect to live under the most ideal environmental
conditions.

Many, if not most, gerontologists agree that the primary determinant
of longevity, that is, how long an organism will live, is its genetic make-up.

Indeed, it has been said that the best way to insure a long life would be to be able to select long-lived parents and grandparents (Dublin, Lotka, and Spiegelman 1949; Wolstenholme and O'Connor 1959).

The mode of action of the hereditary machine is basically the same for all animals. Since a detailed discussion of genetics, the science of inheritance, is beyond the scope of this book, the reader is referred to a good introductory genetics textbook for further details. In the sections which follow, some of the evidence in support of the principle of the *inheritance* of longevity is presented.

Genealogical Studies

Some of the strongest evidence in support of the inheritance of longevity comes from a number of family genealogical studies. For example, Alexander Graham Bell, an amateur genealogist, studied the 2200 male and 1800 female descendants of William Hyde. He found that the children of parents who had both lived beyond the age of 80, had an average life span of 52.7 years, whereas the average life span of children whose parents had both died before the age of 60 was 20 years shorter (Dublin, Lotka, and Spiegelman 1949).

In a more recent study, Jones and coworkers (1956) calculated the potential advantage of having long-lived parents and grandparents. They found that if all four of your grandparents lived to 80 years of age, you could expect to live four years longer than someone whose grandparents did not survive past 60. If your parents both lived past 90 years, you could expect to live seven years longer than someone whose parents died at age 60. Conversely, if neither parent lived past 60 years of age, the child would be expected to die almost two years earlier than one whose parents survived well beyond 60.

Life Insurance Statistics

Practical evidence favoring the hereditary basis for longevity is the fact that life insurance companies place a great deal of emphasis on information concerning the longevity of parents, brothers, and sisters of the person to be insured. Dublin and coworkers (1949) have reported studies by American and Canadian life insurance companies which indicate that death rates are consistently lower for policyholders whose parents both died at later ages than those for persons whose parents died at ages below 50 and 60. A number of other factors are considered in determining the insurability of a person. These include occupation, health, eating and sleeping habits, place of residence, and, of course, the incidence of inheritable family illnesses such as diabetes, high blood pressure, or ulcers. Although they are not part of the normal aging process, such diseases do play a significant role in determining how long a person can live. At the same time, the tendency to inherit such diseases represents, indirectly, a genetic determinant of longevity.

Studies of Twins

Probably the most telling evidence in favor of the genetic determination of longevity comes from studies involving twins. A well-known study by Kallman and Sander (Kallman 1957) involved 687 males and 907 females (or 797 adult twin pairs) over 60 years of age. These included both **identical twins** (which develop from the same egg cell and therefore have an identical genetic make-up) and **fraternal twins** (which develop from two different egg cells and therefore have a different genetic make-up). Regardless of whether they lived in similar or different environments, there was an average difference of 38.5 months between the times of death of the two members of identical twin pairs. On the other hand, fraternal twins died an average of 75.2 months apart, which is almost twice the figure for identical twin pairs.

Several individual cases of a striking similarity in the life spans of identical twins can be cited in this connection. One interesting study involved identical twin sisters. One sister had married a farmer, raised a large family, and had lived the greater part of her adult life in the country. Her sister had remained single and lived in a large city, earning her living as a dressmaker. Both sisters suffered a massive cerebral hemorrhage on the same day at the age of 69; they died 26 days apart. In another case, identical twin brothers who had lived in different cities both died on the very same day at the age of 86.

Species-Specific Longevity

Additional evidence for the genetic determination of longevity is the consistency of length of life within each animal species. For all species of animals which have been studied, the values for mean and maximum longevity within that species remain constant. The values are particularly close within specific strains of different species of animals used in the laboratory, regardless of the laboratories in which they have been maintained, as long as the conditions of maintenance have been essentially the same. Closer to home, the average life expectancy of men and women is very close, if not identical, in virtually all countries of the world (United Nations Demographic Yearbook 1976). Clearly, the data for even the highly hybridized human species indicate a common genetic basis for life span.

Sex Differences and Longevity

Another strong line of evidence supporting the inheritance of longevity is the consistently longer average life span for females than for males among most animal species studied. In the fruit fly, for example, under specific controlled conditions, the female lives an average of 33 days, whereas the male lives an average of only 31 days. Similarly the female rat lives about 900 days, but the male has an average life span of only 750 days. For the human species, in all but 9 countries of the world (Liberia, Nigeria, Upper Volta, Bangladesh, India, Indonesia, Jordan, East Malaysia, and New Guinea), the life expectancy at birth for women is consistently greater than it is for men. Various explanations have been proposed for this sex differential in longevity favoring the female. The most commonly proposed hypothesis is that, in most species, the greater longevity of the female is due to the fact that she possesses a pair of matched sex (XX) chromosomes whereas males have two dissimilar sex chromosomes (X and Y) and, therefore, one less X-chromosome than the female. Whatever the true mechanism involved, there is no question that being female usually means living longer.

Experimental Inbreeding of Longevity

Finally, there is good *experimental* evidence for the inheritance of either short or long life. Long-lived offspring can be produced through selective, genetic inbreeding (i.e., by mating brother and sister, mother and son, or father and daughter). This procedure would be highly desirable in the case of domesticated animals. One set of actual experiments with fruit flies was designed to test this hypothesis. Through many generations of selective inbreeding, five different strains were produced, each with a characteristic mean longevity. These ranged from 14 days for the shortest-lived strain to 44 days for the longest-lived strain. Moreover, once isolated, each strain produced, generation after generation, offspring with the average life span characteristic of the parents of that strain (Pearl and Parker 1922).

Extrinsic Determinants: Environmental Influences on Longevity

As we have seen, heredity is the primary determinant of longevity, providing the genetic program for the maximum potential life span of the individual under optimal environmental conditions. However, adverse environmental influences can play a significant role in shortening one's potential longevity. As early as the prenatal stage, improper maternal diet or the presence of certain drugs in the fetal environment may adversely affect the fetus and eventually reduce what would have been its potential life span. For example, the drug diethylstilbestrol, given to pregnant women to prevent the spontaneous abortion of the fetus in a threatened pregnancy, has been found to cause cancer in the female offspring involved. More obviously, however, once a normal offspring is born, less than ideal environmental conditions can interfere with the full expression of the genetic program for longevity. The advantage of more favorable environments is readily demonstrable. For example, country-dwelling farmers live an average of five years longer than city dwellers. According to the American Cancer Society, a person who smokes two packs of cigarettes per day may expect to live approximately 12 years less than someone who has never smoked. Similarly, as discussed below, married persons have a longer average life span than single, divorced, or widowed individuals. Thus, according to statistics gathered, a married person living in a rural area who is a nonsmoker can expect to live about 22 years longer than a city dweller who smokes, is unmarried, and lives alone. Other adverse environmental factors, such as improper diet, radiation, air pollution, and physical and mental stress, can likewise shorten the genetically programmed or potential life span of any organism, including human beings. Some of the more important environmental factors known through observation or scientific study to modify life span are discussed in greater detail below.

Parental Age

There is some evidence from animal studies that the older the parent at the time of production of the offspring, the shorter the life span of that offspring will be. However, in the case of human beings, there is no direct statistical evidence that the age of the parents at the time of an infant's birth affects the longevity of that child. It is indeed true that there is statistical evidence for the increased incidence of stillbirths, congenital abnormalities (including those of the heart and nervous system), and mongolism among children born of older parents (Miner 1954).

Radiation

Animals subjected to sufficient intensities of **ionizing radiation** (such as X-rays) do in general show shorter life spans than unexposed animals. Autopsies of both exposed and unexposed animals reveal that both groups tend to succumb to similar diseases. However, the animals exposed to ionizing radiation contract degenerative diseases, including cancer, at a much

earlier age than the untreated animals. Ionizing radiation also produces mutations both in the genes of the **germ cells** (the cells that produce the eggs and
sperm) and in the **somatic cells** (all other cells of the body). In the case of
severe damage, the affected cells die very rapidly. However, when such
mutations are not lethal, the resulting altered genetic machinery may ultimately upset normal cell processes, especially protein synthesis. Radiation
may also damage the system responsible for fending off infection, namely, the
body's immune system. Finally, radiation can increase the production of
highly reactive molecules called *free radicals* (discussed in Chapter 4), which
may damage or destroy important structural components of the cells.

Disease

Any one of a number of infectious diseases is capable of appreciably
reducing one's potential life span in a number of ways. For example, rheumatic fever, even as a childhood disease, may result in severe and permanent
damage to the heart. The effect of this damage can increase with age as the
heart continues to weaken over time, so that the life span is drastically short-
ened. Also, as one grows older, one's susceptibility to disease increases and
the ability to survive the stresses associated with disease may also be drastically reduced. Young persons may be less susceptible, for example, to the
common flu virus (influenza) and, even when they do contract the disease,
may show relatively minor symptoms. On the other hand, an older person
may not only more readily contract this disease, but, in most cases, the course
of illness will be more severe. In fact, influenza results in many more fatalities
in older people than in any other segment of the population. For this reason,
immunization programs in the United States, particularly against the more
virulent strains of the influenza virus, usually focus on the elderly.

Marital Status

Marital status is a significant environmental factor in determining the
human life span. Vital statistics show that married people have a longer
average life span than single ones. Similarly, single people live longer than
those who are divorced, and widowed people have the shortest average life
span. A married person has a life expectancy as much as five years greater
than someone who is not married. This may be related to the basic genetic
make-up, which, in turn, may determine one's personality traits and, therefore, the tendency to marry or not. However, in addition to this, there are
many obvious and observable benefits from living with another person in an
ongoing relationship. Married people tend to take better care of themselves

and of one another during their normal daily lives and especially during the illness of one of the pair. Sharing living accommodations has obvious economic advantages which often result in a better diet, better health care, and better living conditions. This is especially true after retirement when limited retirement funds must be stretched. Furthermore, married persons, generally speaking, tend to have more moderate, regularized habits of eating and sleeping and a more regular pattern of social activities. However, the fact that people who are in poor health or who have limited economic means often may not marry (or remarry) is also reflected in these statistics. Such a disadvantaged life style, which itself predicts a relatively shorter life, tends to limit further length of life because of the lesser likelihood of the advantages of marriage.

Longevity statistics favoring married persons may be changing with the times. The increasing number of unmarried couples living together on a longterm basis may also reap the benefits now attributed to marriage. In addition, one important study has shown that the life expectancy of 30,000 Catholic nuns and 10,000 monks age 45 and over was 2.2 years and 1.2 years greater, respectively, than that of noncleric, unmarried men and women who were presumably living alone. In regard to other species, it is interesting to note that the rate of aging (although not necessarily the longevity) of rats kept in cages with other rats (regardless of sex) was found to be slower than that of rats kept in a solitary state under otherwise identical conditions. However, for humans, living with another person or other people, whether in marriage or otherwise, seems to favor greater longevity. Vital statistics of the future may require, therefore, in addition to the traditional categories of "married" and "unmarried," new categories to reflect the emergence of these new facts. (See Dublin et al. 1949; Shurtleff 1955; von Merina and Weniger 1959.)

References

Dublin, L. I., A. J. Lotka, and M. Spiegelman. 1949. Length of life. The Ronald Press, New York. Pp. 99–118.

Jones, H. B. 1956. A special consideration of the aging process, disease and life expectancy. *In* J. H. Lawrence and C. A. Tobias, eds. Advances in biological and medical physics 4:281–337.

Kallman, F. J. 1957. Twin data on the genetics of aging. Pages 131–148 *in* G.E.W. Wolstenholme and C. M. O'Connor, eds. Methodology of the study of aging. Little, Brown and Co., Boston.

Medvedev, Z. A. 1974. Caucasus and Altay longevity: A biological or social problem. The Gerontologist, Oct.: 381–387.

Meyers, R. J. 1966. Validity of centenarian data in the 1960 census. Demography 3:470–476.

Metropolitan Life Insurance Co. 1975. Statistical bulletin. 56 (April): 1–12.

Miner, R. W., ed. 1954. Parental age and characteristics of the offspring. Annals of the New York Academy of Science 57:451.

Pearl, R., and S. L. Parker. 1922. Experimental studies on the duration of life. Amer. Nat. 56:174–187.

Shurtleff, D. 1955. Mortality and marital status. U.S. Public Health Reports 70:248–252.

Siegel, J. S. 1972. Some demographic aspects of aging in the United States. Pages 17–82 *in* A. M. Ostfield and D. C. Gibson, eds., Epidemiology of aging. National Institute of Child Health and Human Development NIH 77–711. U.S. Dept. of Health, Education and Welfare, Bethesda, Md.

United Nations. 1976. Demographic yearbook. New York.

Von Merina, O., and F. L. Weniger. 1959. Social-cultural background of the aging individual. Pages 279–335 *in* J. E. Birren, ed. Handbook of aging and the individual. University of Chicago Press.

Wolstenholme, G.E.W., and M. O'Connor, eds. 1959. The lifespan of animals. Little, Brown and Co., Boston. 324 pp.

Chapter Four

Theories of Aging

We have seen that human beings, like all other animals studied, have a distinct species-specific average life span as well as a maximum life span. Aging, however, is not a simple statistic like longevity. It is instead a complex, multifaceted process that, in a highly hybridized species like the human being, proceeds at different rates in various organs in any one individual as well as at different rates for the same organ in different persons. The complexity of the process perhaps explains why there are more than a half-dozen theories or hypotheses of aging, each based, generally, on one particular aspect of the aging process. Indeed, a single holistic theory of aging, which is applicable to all organs or even to the average aging individual, is still difficult to formulate. Nevertheless, the universality of the aging process justifies the continued attempt of the research scientist to find a common underlying basis for this process. In fact, the major aims of the gerontologist are, as we have said, to determine (1) the facts of aging and (2) the mechanisms or causes underlying this universal biological phenomenon. This knowledge can aid practicing geriatricians—physicians, nurses, counsellors, social workers, and paramedics—in their task of making "living longer better."

A number of the currently proposed theories have a common underlying theme. That is that aging of organs and, ultimately, of the entire body is a programmed process. The alternative proposal is that aging is nothing more than the accumulation with time of insults from the environment either internal or external in nature. Perhaps closer to the truth is the likelihood that the aging process represents a cumulative, age-related summation of the inherited program for aging, combined with the effect of accumulating environmental insults suffered by an individual from infancy through old age.

Any theory of aging must meet the following three criteria:

1. The aging phenomenon under consideration must be evident universally in all members of a given species.

2. The process must be progressive with time.
3. The process must be deleterious in nature, leading ultimately to the failure of the organ or system.

The Programmed Theory

Wilson (1974) has stressed that aging must be a programmed process, since each species shows a predictable species-specific pattern of changes in the body as it grows older. He proposes that such a process, leading ultimately to the failure of the individual to survive, has evolved to maximize the survival of each species. Thus, after having fulfilled their role of propagating a new generation, the adults eventually undergo a program of aging which has been established by evolution. The death of most of the adults at a given average age then permits the survival of the new generation for the purpose of propagation and perpetuation of the species. The main criticism of this theory of programmed aging is that it only explains the *why* and not the *how* (i.e., the mechanisms or causes) of aging.

The Gene Theory

This is an essentially fatalistic theory of aging as a programmed process which has a number of variations. Most simply, it proposes the existence within each organism of one or more deleterious genes which become active late in life and result in the organism's failure to survive. A variation on this theme is the concept that there are two kinds of genes for aging, the favorable (juvenescent) genes, responsible for youthful vigor and mature adult well-being, and the unfavorable (senescent) genes, responsible for functional decline and structural deterioration. During early life, the juvenescent genes predominate, and the senescent genes then begin to take over in early middle age and predominate thereafter. A third variation proposes that one set of genes serves a dual role which, early in life, is favorable but which, in middle age and later, becomes unfavorable. Genes having such a dual role, as it were, are termed **pleiotrophic.** An example cited of the functioning of pleiotrophic genes is the age-related, genetically determined pattern of reproductive function in the human female. Thus, the hormone **estrogen** is responsible for the normal reproductive cycle in women and, therefore, essential to reproduction of the species. At the same time, this hormone is said to reduce the likelihood of **arteriosclerosis** (and, therefore, high blood pressure) in the premenopausal woman. Yet, with the onset of menopause, a truly programmed phenomenon, the marked concomitant reduction in estrogen production makes the late middle-aged female more susceptible to arteriosclerosis.

Whether or not one accepts the gene theory of programmed senescence as the basis for aging either wholly or in part, considering the complexity of this process from organ to organ, one must at least postulate that it must involve *many* genes.

The Running-Out-of-Program Theory

This popular theory postulates that, at fertilization, each cell of the offspring is endowed with only a given amount of genetic material. Thus, as cells grow old, the basic genetic material of the nucleus, that is, the **DNA,** is ultimately used up and the cells fail. This concept is supported in part by numerous reports of a gradual, age-related diminution of activity or amount of certain **enzymes** (catalysts of cellular activity) in such organs as the liver, brain, and muscle of lower mammals. (See also the discussion of the Error Theory on page 42.)

Other support for this theory was provided by Hayflick and his colleagues (1974) who studied aging of living cells maintained in cultures outside the body (*in vitro*). Allowed to thrive and multiply in appropriate nutrient media and under sterile conditions, cells from human lung tissues, for example, multiply rapidly, at first doubling every 24 hours. However, as this process progresses, the time between successive doublings increases. Thus, after about 50 doublings (or about 6 months) the cells fail to double and the cell strain dies out. This clearly suggests that the capability for such cells to divide diminishes over time. The same phenomenon has been repeatedly observed not only in a variety of other human and other animal tissues cultured *in vitro,* but also in single-celled animals like *Paramecium* (Siegel 1967). In the latter case, it has been shown that, regardless of continued subculturing under standardized conditions, *Paramecium* will undergo only a definitive number of cell divisions, after which no further reproduction by this means is possible. (For further discussions of these studies, see Hayflick 1974 and Siegel 1967.) Related to the Hayflick phenomenon is the fact that **connective tissue** cells (*fibroblasts*) taken from young persons suffering from the disease *progeria,*[1] when cultured *in vitro,* will double only as few as 2 and not more than 30 times before the culture dies out. This evidence from *cytogerontology,* the study of aging in cells, certainly suggests that, in some tissues at least, aging is indeed a programmed phenomenon in which either the cells or important components of the cell can be replaced only so many times.

[1]A fairly rare disease involving premature aging, in which children show all the classical, external signs of advanced age, including wrinkled skin, gray hair, and feeble movements.

The Somatic Mutation Theory

For the most part, this theory is based on studies by the late biochemist, H. J. Curtis. With his colleagues he found that, by exposing mice and guinea pigs to X-rays or by the direct application to the liver of certain chemicals like carbon tetrachloride, a considerable number of liver cells were destroyed. When these cells were replaced by cell division of the remaining cells, which were apparently injured, the new liver cells produced had a high incidence of abnormal chromosomes (the cell structures that carry the genes). Furthermore, examination of liver cells from *untreated* mice revealed a greater incidence of such chromosomal abnormalities in older mice compared to liver cells from young mice. Similarly, cells from the liver of mice of a short-lived strain showed an appreciably greater incidence of such chromosomal aberrations *at any age* compared to liver cells from a long-lived strain of mice of a comparable age. In fact, liver cells from the *youngest* of short-lived mice consistently showed a higher incidence of such abnormalities than cells from even the *oldest* mice of the long-lived strain. On the basis of this evidence, Curtis and his followers proposed that aging of all cells in the senescent animal is the result of the time-dependent accumulation of such chromosomal aberrations (or *somatic mutations*), regardless of the cause.

The Cross-Linkage Theory

The cross-linkage theory was proposed over 25 years ago by Johan Bjorksten, an industrial polymer chemist concerned with long-chain compounds like nylon and polyesters. The theory was based on his observation that the protein gelatin used in the Ditto machine, an early copy machine, was irreversibly altered, or *denatured,* by chemicals such as formaldehyde. Therefore, he proposed that irreversible aging of proteins like **collagen**[2] is responsible for the ultimate failure of tissues and organs in relation to age. The proponents of this theory (see Bjorksten 1974) suggest that the known accumulation of numerous cross-linking compounds produce the random, irreparable binding together of essential molecules in the cells, ranging from the DNA within the nucleus to collagen as a supportive element. This then results in the disturbance of normal cell functioning, the cross-linked network impeding intracellular transport or producing changes in the DNA responsible for protein synthesis in general and normal immunological function in particular.

[2]Collagen is an important supportive component forming part of the framework of the lungs, heart, muscle, and the lining of the walls of blood vessels. It literally holds the cells of these important body tissues together. Changes in its structure with age are in part responsible for the condition of arteriosclerosis and the concomitant loss of elasticity of blood vessels in older persons.

The Free Radical Theory

The free radical theory is really a special case of the cross-linkage theory. However, instead of accepting a wide range of noxious compounds which can produce cross linkage, *free radicals* are identified as the cause of aging. Free radicals are chemical components of the cell which arise as a by-product of normal cell processes produced by the action of oxygen. They exist for only very brief periods (a second or less), since they are highly reactive chemically with other substances, especially **unsaturated fats.** Because the envelope of the cell, its *membrane,* is made up in part of such fatty or **lipid** substances, it can be readily damaged and then become "leaky" if subjected to an excessive number of accumulating free radicals. Free radicals may also cause mutations of chromosomes and thus damage the basic normal genetic machinery. Most serious of all is the fact that free radicals are self-propagating. That is, as a free radical reacts with a molecule, it is capable of releasing several new free radicals, themselves capable of producing new free radicals, thus producing more damage and even more numbers of damaging free radicals in their turn. The fact that naturally occurring **antioxidants** (compounds preventing oxidation processes) like vitamins C and E can reduce or inhibit the production of new free radicals has been the basis for the recent popular argument that these vitamins can extend life span. It is interesting to note that BHT (butylated hydroxytoluene), a common food preservative, is an antioxidant and free-radical inhibitor. Fed to mice, it has been shown to extend their life span significantly. As for humans, further studies are required before such antioxidants can be promoted as having life-prolonging properties.

The Clinker Theory

This theory can be considered either independently or as a variation of the somatic mutation, cross-linkage, and free radical theories of aging (discussed above). It suggests that aging is a reflection of the time-related accumulation of deleterious substances within various cells of the body. These would include a number of chemical by-products of cellular metabolism (such as lipofuscin, **histones, aldehydes, quinones** and free radicals), which are known to accumulate in increasing quantities within the **cytoplasm** of most cells. Most notable of these is the group of golden-brown pigments known as lipofuscins. These are *inert* substances, that is, they are chemically inert and do not have the ability to react with other substances, and they are known to accumulate with time in a number of organs, including the heart, skeletal muscle, brain, and other nerve tissues. (See *lipofuscin* in the Glossary.) It has been suggested that the accumulation of such inert substances interferes with the normal functioning of such tissues by a displacement of otherwise functional cytoplasmic components of the cells involved. On the other hand, substances (like free radicals and histones) known to produce irreversible changes in the cellular components, including denaturation of **proteins,** are seen to be responsible for aging in terms of the ultimate functional decline of an increasing number of cells as such substances accumulate with advancing age.

The Error Theory

This popular but relatively unsubstantiated theory proposes that, as cells continue to function, random errors may occur somewhere in the process of the synthesis of new proteins. Protein synthesis involves a complex series of steps, beginning with the DNA in the nucleus and the **transcription** of the genetic code, and leading in the ultimate **translation** of the code in the final steps to the production of protein. The process also involves important cell components called *enzymes,* catalysts which are responsible for all cellular activities. Random errors could also occur in the synthesis of those enzymes which are themselves concerned with the synthesis of other proteins; this would accelerate the accumulation of errors. With time, the result would be a decrease in protein synthesis to a catastrophic failing level.

This theory addresses the question of the cause of aging simply on the basis of the time-related failure of protein synthesis due to such errors. However, a number of recent studies have failed to show any *qualitative* changes in the enzymes studied, although in each case the enzymes did show a decrease in *activity* with advancing age. Thus, the concept of the failure of protein biosynthetic mechanisms through *errors* as a basis for universal cellular senescence cannot be the complete answer to why the cells of organisms grow old.

The Wear and Tear Theory

This theory involves the concept that aging is a programmed process, but stresses that cells are continuously wearing out, very much like a machine, with the wear and tear of extended usage. The process is aggravated by the harmful effects of internal and external stress factors, including the accumulation of injurious by-products of metabolism (see the Clinker Theory, p. 41). The accumulation of such combined damage to the cell contents with age, along with the increasing failure of the cells to repair or replace damaged vital cellular components, causes cell death in increasing numbers with advancing age.

The process of aging in two of the most important tissues of the body—namely, the striated skeletal and heart muscles and all of the nerve cells, including those of the brain—lends support to the wear and tear theory. These two types of so-called **postmitotic** tissues are unique in that they are incapable of undergoing cell division. Muscle fibers and nerve cells are, therefore, unable to replace cells when they are destroyed due to wear and tear or to specific mechanical or chemical injury.

The Autoimmune Theory

This theory, originally proposed by Walford (1969) and more recently supported by Adler (1974), simply states that aging is the consequence of development of **autoimmunity,** or self-attack, as it were, by the organism's immune system, which was designed by nature to repel or overcome bacterial or viral infection or invasion by foreign proteins. From birth, the body's immune system has "memorized" the structural configuration of its own thousands and thousands of proteins, which it continues to recognize at least through middle age. Accordingly, in the normal young person or healthy adult, the immune system will repel or attack only foreign proteins through the production of antibodies or attack by certain white blood cells. The autoimmune theory proposes that, with advancing age, defects arise in the immune system so that *self* cannot be distinguished from *not-self* (i.e., foreign structures). The production of antibodies to *self* results.

The autoimmune theory attempts to explain *what* happens in the aging of the immune system, but it does not explain *how* it happens. An explanation either in terms of genetic errors, somatic mutation, or cross linkage of normal molecules concerned with antibody production is needed for a more complete understanding of how the body ages.

Summary

The newcomer to the field of gerontology may be understandably overwhelmed by the number and variety of theories of aging which have been proposed by different scientists. This chapter has attempted to summarize the more commonly discussed and seemingly plausible theories. However, it is obvious that no single theory proposed to date adequately explains the complex and heterogeneous sets of events which we call the aging process. Indeed, it is easier to visualize how several processes, mutually interacting and each described by a separate theory, might produce many different kinds of time-dependent changes that we collectively call "aging". For example, a genetic program for the maximum length of life for an individual could be considered as determining the rate, direction, and extent of the aging process, whether we are speaking of organs or of the whole organism. Superimposed upon this primary determinant would be its modification by the wear and tear upon the organism produced by daily environmental stresses, by cellular mutations of important systems, or by the cross linking of large molecules, all further reducing the functional capacities of the various major organ systems of the body. Similarly, the later development of an autoimmune system, whether by free radicals and cross-linking compounds or through errors in the synthesis of protein antibodies, would augment the genetic program for aging inherited by the organism in question.

In summary, then, no one theory of aging proposed thus far is capable of adequately explaining the polyphasic, complex process of growing old, despite the fact that each theory proposed appears to have considerable merit as it applies to specific observations of age-related changes in particular organs or systems.

References

Adler, W. H. 1974. An "autoimmune" theory of aging. Pages 33–42 *in* M. Rockstein, M. L. Sussman, and J. Chesky, eds. Theoretical aspects of aging. Academic Press, New York.

Bjorksten, J. 1974. Crosslinkage and the aging process. Pages 43–59 *in* M. Rockstein, M. L. Sussman, and J. Chesky, eds. Theoretical aspects of aging.

Crowley, C., and H. J. Curtis. 1963. The development of somatic mutations in mice with age. Proceedings of the National Academy of Sciences 49:626–628.

Curtis, H. J., and K. Miller. 1971. Chromosome aberrations in liver cells of guinea pigs. Journal of Gerontology 26:292–294.

Gordon, P. 1974. Free radicals and the aging process. Pages 61–81 *in* M. Rockstein, M. L. Sussman, and J. Chesky, eds. Theoretical aspects of aging.

Hayflick, L. 1974. Cytogerontology. Pages 83–103 *in* M. Rockstein, M. L. Sussman, and J. Chesky, eds. Theoretical aspects of aging.

Siegel, R. W. 1967. Genetics of aging and the life cycle in ciliates. Proceedings of the Society of Experimental Biology 21:127–148.

Walford, R. L. 1969. The immunological theory of aging. Williams and Wilkins, Baltimore.

Wilson, D. L. 1974. The programmed theory of aging. Pages 11–21 *in* M. Rockstein, M. L. Sussman, and J. Chesky, eds. Theoretical aspects of aging.

Chapter Five

The Nervous System

We begin our survey of the age-related changes in the various organ systems of the human body with the nervous system because it coordinates the activities of all the other organ systems of the body. Loss of nervous system functions is perhaps the most frightening aspect of aging to many people, as one envisions spending the last years of one's life as a tottering, trembling, disoriented person who may also have lost control over the salivary, urinary, or bowel functions. Moreover, because of the recent redefinition of death as the cessation of brain function (confirmed in many cases by the absence of characteristic electrical wave patterns charted by the electroencephalogram), the functioning of the nervous system has assumed even greater importance today.

In this chapter we will examine the specific changes that have been found to take place in the nervous system with aging and how these may affect the functioning and behavior of an elderly person. After a brief survey of the organization and general functions of the components of the nervous system, we will note the changes that occur at the most basic level—that of the cell. These include losses in cell number and changes in the composition and structure of the cells. We will examine how certain changes in the brain may be accompanied by a decline in intelligence and memory in the normal aging process, and how disease states, specifically organic brain syndrome and stroke, particularly affect the aged. The effect of aging on the involuntary functions of the body are discussed in relation to the autonomic nervous system and the reflexes. Finally, the important changes in the senses, such as vision and hearing, and their effect on the daily lives of the elderly will be examined.

Organization and General Function

All forms of life have had to develop some means of remaining in contact with the world around them; that is, the organism must have the ability to identify and to respond to appropriate elements in the particular environment in which it lives. In the simplest multicellular animals, such as fresh and salt water invertebrates, the nervous system is represented by a network of undifferentiated cells. The most highly organized nervous system is found in the higher mammals, as exemplified particularly in human beings. The basic organization of the nervous system involves (1) the **central nervous system,** (2) the **autonomic nervous system,** and (3) the sensory cells and sense organs. The fundamental unit of structure and function of the nervous system is the nerve cell.

Nerve Cells

The **neuron** or nerve cell is the basic unit of structure and function of the nervous system. As shown in Figure 5.1, a typical neuron is a rather unusual-looking cell. As in all other cells, the cell body contains the cytoplasm and the nucleus. However, unlike most other cells, a neuron's cytoplasm and its outer cell membrane are extended into *processes,* called *fibers.* In most cases, a relatively longer, single fiber, called an **axon,** conducts nerve impulses away from the cell body. Shorter, finer fibers, called **dendrites,** conduct nerve impulses from outside of the cell towards the cell body. The longer axons are generally grouped in bundles. When serving as connecting or transmitting nerves *within* the central nervous system they are called *tracts.* Bundles of such fibers located *outside* of the central nervous system, however, are called **nerves.** **Sensory nerves** are those which contain fibers arising from sensory cells, and carry **afferent** (incoming) impulses into the central nervous system. **Motor nerves** are those containing fibers arising in motor cells within the central nervous system and which ultimately produce an excitatory or inhibitory effect upon muscles or glands.

The Central Nervous System: The Brain and Spinal Cord

The *brain* is encased by the skull and is connected directly to the *spinal cord.* The largest part of the brain, the **cerebrum** (Fig. 5.2), is more highly developed in humans than in all other animals. The estimated 14 billion neurons (nerve cells) of the cerebrum are located in its outer layer, the **cortex.** Neurophysiological and anatomical studies have established areas in the cortex associated with three major functions. The *motor cortex* coordinates voluntary movements of the body through direct action on the *skeletal muscle.* The *sensory cortex* is the center of *perception,* or the recognition of changes in the environment, which we call vision, hearing, smell, taste, touch, and pain.

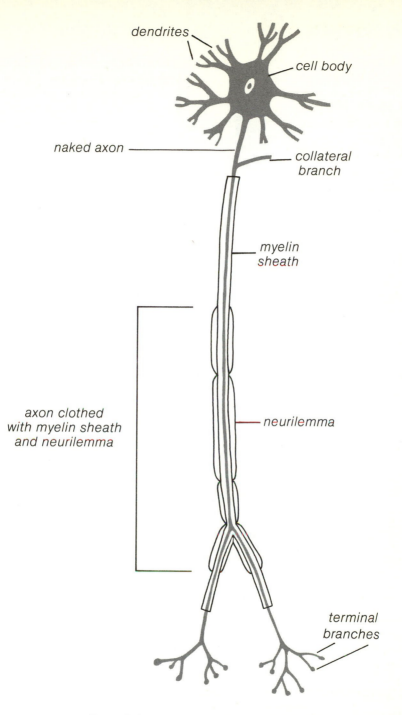

dendrites

cell body

naked axon

collateral
branch

myelin
sheath

axon clothed
with myelin sheath
and neurilemma

neurilemma

terminal
branches

Figure 5.1.   A nerve cell. (After Stöhr.)

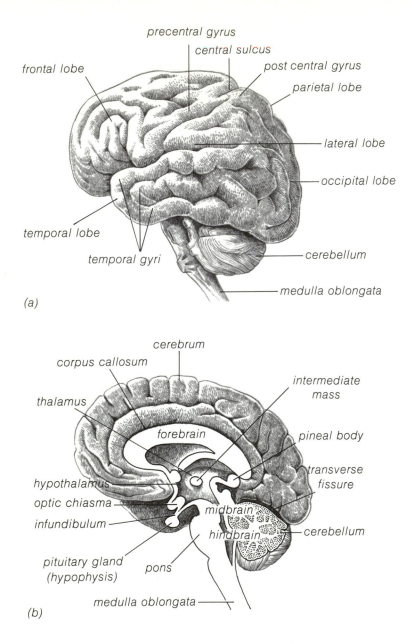

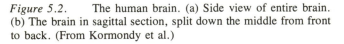

Figure 5.2.   The human brain. (a) Side view of entire brain. (b) The brain in sagittal section, split down the middle from front to back. (From Kormondy et al.)

The *associational cortex* includes those areas involved in the *cognitive functions,* (reasoning, abstract thinking, and memory) as well as consciousness in general.

The *spinal cord* represents the original, older, more primitive nervous system, the anterior part of which has become highly organized and developed into the mass of cells and their fibers which we call the brain. It consists of 31 segments of nervous tissue, each containing a pair of *spinal nerves* (Fig. 5.3a). The gray matter of the spinal cord, also made up of neurons, is internally located and has roughly the form of the letter H (Fig. 5.3b).

The spinal cord is primarily a massive column of **nerve fibers** organized into groups called **nerve tracts.** It serves as a series of pathways which connect the higher and lower segments of the central nervous system (including the brain) with both incoming sensory nerve fibers and outgoing motor nerve fibers arising in distinct areas of the central nervous system. The spinal cord is also the center for important **reflexes** involving skeletal muscle reactions, such as the knee jerk.

The Autonomic Nervous System

The *autonomic nervous system* is essentially one of outgoing or **efferent** nerve fibers, which arise from motor neurons in the lower part of the brain and in the spinal cord. Its two divisions, the *sympathetic* and *parasympathetic* divisions, are distinguishable both anatomically and physiologically. The nerves of the sympathetic division originate in the cells of each of the spinal cord segments beginning with the first *thoracic* and ending with the fourth lumbar regions (Fig. 5.4). The *parasympathetic* nerves arise from the brain below the cortex and from the last three (*sacral*) segments of the spinal cord. Thus, the parasympathetic division is also referred to as the *craniosacral* division of the autonomic nervous system.

The autonomic nervous system is also called the *involuntary* or vegetative nervous system because it is involved in the control of activities which are not ordinarily subject to voluntary or conscious control. It controls the contraction of all of the involuntary muscles in the body, such as those in the gut and the walls of blood vessels. It also regulates the release of **secretions** from the many glands in the body. The diameter of the eye's iris, the rate of heartbeat, the force of the heart's contraction, breathing, sneezing, coughing, and the secretion by the digestive and sweat glands are all under the control of this system. Paling or flushing of the skin and urinary or bowel continence are likewise typical involuntary activities under its control. With few exceptions, the actions of the two divisions of the autonomic nervous system are mutually

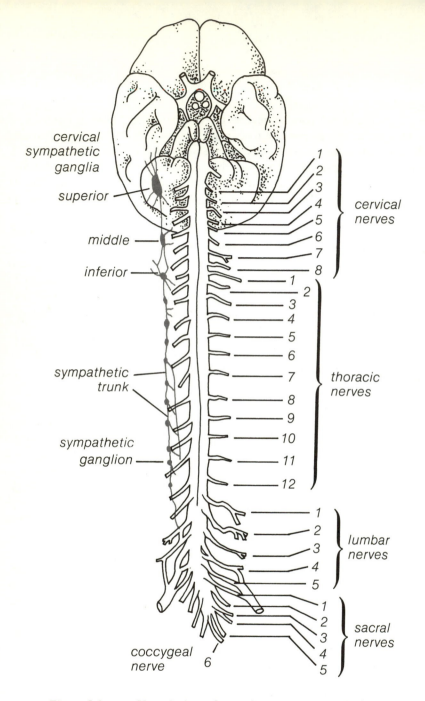

Figure 5.3a. Ventral view of central nervous system (brain and spinal cord), showing sympathetic chain. (After Morris.)

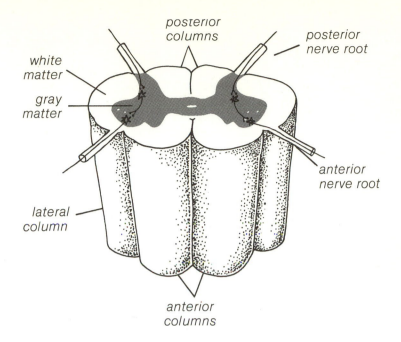

Figure 5.3b.   A cross-section of the spinal cord showing the central gray matter and the outer columns of white matter.

antagonistic. For example, parasympathetic nerve impulses slow and weaken the force of the heartbeat, whereas sympathetic nerve impulses to the heart increase rate and force of contraction, or *stroke volume*. Their interaction tends to maintain the appropriate level of the heart's pumping effectiveness (see Chapter 6) in one's daily activities.

The body's involuntary responses to emergency signals and to emotional and physical stress are also under the control of the autonomic nervous system. For example, the dilation of the pupils, the release of glucose (a simple sugar) for energy from the liver, and the acceleration and increased force of the heartbeat in response to fear or anger are the kinds of rapid responses of the body to stress that are mediated through the autonomic nervous system. Other similar responses under the control of this system are shivering and increased metabolism when the body is exposed to *lowering* ambient temperatures. Conversely, sweating and auxiliary circulatory changes effecting increased heat loss are augmented in the face of *rising* ambient temperatures.

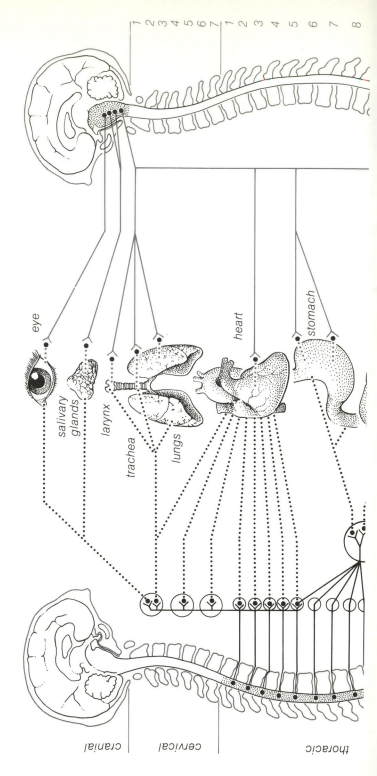

eye

salivary glands

larynx

trachea

lungs

heart

stomach

cranial

cervical

thoracic

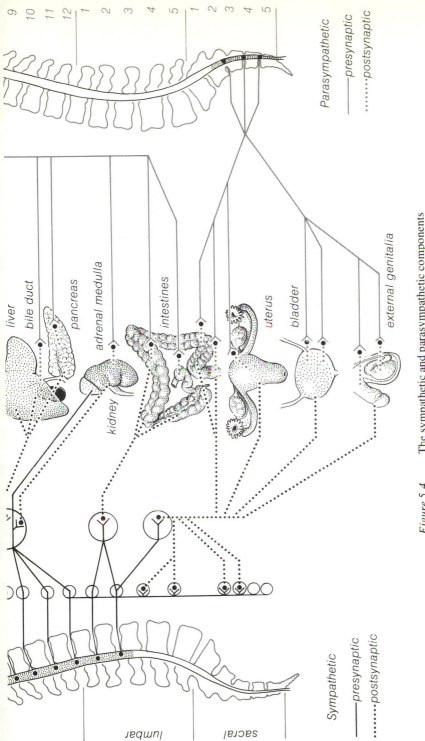

Figure 5.4. The sympathetic and parasympathetic components of the autonomic nervous system. (From Kormondy et al.)

Sensory Cells and Sense Organs

This widely scattered and highly diversified part of the nervous system, located outside of the central nervous system, consists of cells or groups of cells with fairly specific sensitivities to different kinds of environmental stimuli. When sensory (*receptor*) cells are organized with other tissues into specialized structures like the eye or ear, they are termed *sense organs*. Thus, light, pressure, or pain is perceived in the cerebrum as a result of the sensitivity of receptor elements, located within the skin or within the body, that are particularly sensitive to one or the other of these two types of environmental changes. By the same token, neuronal elements in the eye or the inner ear, respectively, are peculiarly adapted to stimulation by light (electromagnetic) waves or pressure changes (sound) in the atmosphere. We are limited in our ability to appreciate sounds above or below a certain frequency range because of the absence of appropriate sensory cells in the inner ear, and normally we can see only a limited range of light wave lengths, because of the limited sensitivity of appropriate sensory elements in the eye which they stimulate. Nevertheless, in general, the sense organs serve us well in analyzing most of the phenomena in the external world with which we come in contact. As we shall see below, age-dependent changes in the number of nerve cells can lead to serious deficits in hearing and vision, and in other senses. This, in turn, may result in significant alterations of behavior in otherwise normal older individuals.

Cellular Changes in Aging

Otherwise healthy people show characteristic and commonly observable changes in the structure and function of the nervous system with age, particularly at the cellular level.

Cell Number

As we mentioned earlier, for all animals studied, nerve cells are unable to undergo cell division once their development is complete. Accordingly, nerve cells lost after their postdevelopmental period cannot be replaced. Thus, during the normal course of aging, many nerve cells die and disappear each day. In the human brain, especially between the ages of 50 and 90, this is especially marked in certain parts of the cerebral cortex. As we shall see in greater detail below, there is a definite loss in *brain mass* beginning after the age of 20 to 30 in the human male and after the age of 18 to 20 in the human female.

On the other hand, some regions of the central nervous system do not exhibit drastic reductions in the number of nerve cells with age. For example, there is no significant change from birth to old age in the number of cells corresponding to the various nerves of the brain (i.e., the *cranial* nerves, including the *facial* and *cochlear* nerves).

Microscopic Changes

In addition to the gross changes in cell number and tissue mass which accompany aging, the cells which remain may show drastically altered structural characteristics with advancing age. Most noticeable is the shrinkage of some cells and the swelling of others, depending upon the part of the nervous system studied. The *cytoplasm,* the major, viscous, (almost fluid) component of the cell, shows increasing accumulation of fatty substances and of cavities of fluid called **vacuoles.** There are also marked changes in the staining properties of the cytoplasm. Moreover, in certain regions of the gray matter of the brain, a characteristic deposition of silver-staining or **argyrophilic plaques** occurs in the brain cells of as many as 84 percent of specimens obtained from deceased persons 65 years of age and over.

Aging Pigments

The outer cortex of the brain takes on a yellow-brown coloration with advancing age. Similarly, the white matter (consisting mainly of nerve fibers) becomes cream colored. These color changes are due to the gradual time-dependent accumulation of yellowish pigments collectively called *lipofuscin* (also termed *lipochromes*). These so-called wear-and-tear or old-age pigments have been reported to occur in nerve and numerous other tissues in almost all animal species which have been studied. Although no single histochemical method[1] can be employed to identify this pigment, it is known to be a heterogeneous chemical compound of lipid, carbohydrate, and protein. Although it may be rare or absent in some cells of the nervous system, it has been observed to appear in some cells of the human brain as early as three months of age. By 12 years of age, all of these cells contain *some* lipofuscin. Thereafter, more and more pigment fills each cell, so that in the brain of a 32-year-old person, 84 perent of the cells are so filled with lipofuscin as to force the nucleus to an eccentric sideward position (Brody 1970). However, there was no significant decrease in cell number of this part of the brain. Since it is generally agreed that reduction with age of functional capacity of the

---

[1] A laboratory procedure for the study of cells, which includes chemical staining and examination of the cells and their contents.

brain is due to the progressive loss of functional cells, the biological significance of the accumulation of this aging pigment in nerve cells in general is still highly debatable.

Nerve Fibers

Associated with both loss in cell number and intracellular changes with age are sizeable losses in the numbers of fibers (usually *axons*) in the nerves outside of the central nervous system. Examples are the *sciatic nerve,* which innervates the back and leg in both humans and rats, and the human *optic* and *vestibular nerves.*

Physiologically, there is limited evidence that the rate of conduction of impulses within nerves decreases with advancing age. However, transmission from neuron to neuron, especially over multineuronal pathways, has definitely been shown to be slower in older rats. Such changes may be a partial cause of the reduced speed of psychomotor responses of older persons (Welford 1959).

Aging of the Central Nervous System

Brain Mass

As has been indicated earlier, the **atrophy** of the brain with advancing age has been amply documented in studies reporting a generalized reduction in its mass (weight) from young to old animals and humans as well. In the human male, the approximate weight of the mature brain between 20 to 30 years of age (when peak weight occurs) is about 1380 grams (about 3 lbs.). A brain from an 80-year-old man, however, weighs about 1240 grams, which is a decrease of about 10 percent in total weight. In extreme cases, several specimens obtained from men over 90 years of age weighed over 20 percent less than those of 20-year-old males. The brain of the human female, which is an average of 100 to 150 grams lighter at all ages, exhibits similar trends toward weight loss, but the loss begins about a decade earlier, at 60 to 70 years of age. This may be due to the fact that the weight of the female brain also peaks a decade earlier, at 18 to 20 years of age. There is also a reduction in brain weight in some lower animals (such as cats, dogs, and guinea pigs) amounting to a 5 to 13 percent decrease in brain weight from youth to old age.

Brain Function

Intelligence.   Accompanying the known onset of loss in brain mass beginning at the mature age of 30, some facets of learning new skills, particularly psychomotor skills, show a definite age-related decline. Indeed, a number of studies clearly indicate that speed of response and perceptual-integrative ability show a far greater decline with age than do verbal ability and ability to store information (Birren 1959; Birren and Schaie 1977). However, decline in intelligence in the elderly is such a widely accepted phenomenon that most tests of intelligence are corrected for age. Thus it is considered normal for an elderly person to have a 7 to 27 percent reduction in verbal ability and a 26 to 50 percent reduction in motor performance ability when compared with a young mature adult of 30.

Such generalizations concerning the decline of certain intellectual functions in old age are based particularly on cross-sectional studies involving averaging of data for individuals selected from different age groups. However, longitudinal studies in which each individual is followed over a fairly long period of time (10 or 20 years, if possible) clearly show a wide variability from individual to individual as to the changes in intellect with age. However, as we shall note from time to time in future chapters dealing with biological aging, certain behavioral concomitants of biological aging tend to be a reflection of the earlier history or life style of the older individual. Thus, for example, intellectual ability in well-educated people tends to remain relatively undiminished in comparison to those with limited educational background. There is also a positive statistical association between a high degree of intelligence and long life in humans. Thus, college graduates and honor students live longer than others, and people listed in *Who's Who* tend to live longer than those who are not. Supreme Court Justices have a longer life expectancy than Congressional or Cabinet members, in that order. (See Verwoerdt 1976 for further details.)

Declining cognitive function may be one of a number of important clinical signs of illness and, at the same time, a prediction of life shortening. A marked, rapid decline in intelligence test scores or other traditional measurements of mental ability and cognitive function may be caused by an underlying disease state. For example, it is not unusual to find a decline in intelligence test scores accompanying high blood pressure in the elderly.

Memory.   Memory (the faculty of recall or remembering) is defined as the ability to reproduce and identify what has been experienced or learned before. Thus, memory is a complex function which includes learning, retention, and either recall or recognition. Both in psychological and ecological terms, memory is a conscious mental event involving the interaction of individuals with their environment, particularly through sensory input and through response by the body through the central nervous system.

In relation to the aging process, one must distinguish between two distinct types of memory. Longterm recollection of events experienced in the distant past is referred to as *longterm memory,* whereas *short-term memory* concerns experiences of the immediate past—usually hours, days, or weeks at most. Even in otherwise healthy older persons, longterm memory appears to be much more vivid; events of long ago are more easily recalled than recent experiences. Whether or not this is a matter of motivation and attitude or a distinct reflection of biological aging has not been established. However, in the case of **senile dementia** (see Organic Brain Syndrome below) an older person can vividly recall such things as the color of the dress her child wore on an Easter Sunday many years ago or the names of friends from high school days, but may have difficulty remembering what was served for breakfast that very morning. Memory loss, the lessening of the ability to recollect past experiences, nevertheless, is a slow, gradual process and is known to occur over a number of decades, unless accelerated by illness or direct physical damage to the brain or to cerebral circulation. For example, memory loss can result from high fever or from the toxic effects of kidney failure upon the brain. A reduction in, or total lack of, oxygen supply to the brain for extended periods of time, which can result from barbiturate overdose, asphyxiation, or extended submersion in water (partial drowning), may likewise adversely affect memory and, indeed, all other cognitive functions, regardless of age.

A number of specialists in the field of neurology and psychiatry have related mild to moderate decline with age in the capacity to remember to the decrease in brain weight and the number of nerve cells. Postmortem studies on persons who were apparently mentally competent at death showed cortical cell losses of under 50 percent and brain weight decreases of not more than 8 percent. Goldfarb (1975) observed that reductions in brain weight in men occur to the extent of 6 percent in the eighth decade, of over 12 percent in the ninth decade, and of 20 percent in the tenth decade of life. At the same time, he suggested that the 6 percent brain weight loss is associated with *mild to moderate* memory loss, over 12 percent with *moderate* memory loss, and 20 percent with *severe* memory loss.

In general, people with more education and those in white collar and professional occupations generally exhibit better memory in old age than those with less education and with lower occupational status. In addition, people who continue to work at their occupations in later life or who occupy their retirement time with comparable volunteer activities also show better recall when tested than people who do retire and fail to maintain interest in challenging outside activities. Finally, it should be emphasized that more complex material tends to be forgotten earlier than simpler items by persons of advanced age. At the same time, psychomotor skills, such as typing or playing a musical instrument, which are learned in youth are more readily re-learned than those learned in later life (and then forgotten).

The Pathogeric Brain

Organic Brain Syndrome.   A common problem in evaluating "normal" aging of the central nervous system is that of distinguishing between what is truly normal and what is secondary to age-related disease. Indeed, nearly 90 percent of all men and women in the United States over the age of 75 exhibit atherosclerosis in the blood vessels to the brain (Finch 1977). It is therefore difficult to distinguish normal changes in function of the brain from those which are consequences of such cerebral **vascular** disease.

Organic brain syndrome is a generic term which includes a variety of pathological states involving the brain, including *senile* and *presenile dementia*. The outward signs of such diseased states of the brain include impairment in orientation, intellect, judgement, and memory. These manifestations of impaired brain function are often accompanied by neurotic or psychotic disorders of affect and behavior. Unfortunately, the etiology of organic brain syndrome usually involves one, frequently more than one, factor (i.e., is multifactorial). Indeed moderate to severe organic brain syndrome (OBS) has been estimated to occur in over 2 percent of the elderly population at large, with a much higher percentage (about 80 percent) in that age group which is institutionalized in psychiatric hospitals. In residential, longterm care institutions such as nursing homes, about two-thirds of residents 65 years and older are diagnosed as having this condition. However, some experts believe that OBS tends to be overdiagnosed in older persons. This may be due in part to the fact that diagnoses are made on the basis of behavioral manifestations, since it has not been possible to date to identify any particular organic brain syndrome with specific organic changes in the brain itself.

The degeneration of the fine elements (the *fibrils*) of the nerve fibers of the brain cells is not a constant feature of aging, although it is a characteristic of some diseases, like **Alzheimer's disease.** Thus, out of 150 psychotic cases involving older persons, only 38 percent of the males and 56 percent of the females showed such neurofibrillar degeneration. Similarly, the accumulation of *senile plaques* in brain cells occurred in only 54 percent of the males and 77 percent of the females in the same study of 150 cases of senile psychoses. In fact, both plaques and neurofibrillar degeneration were absent in 30 percent of the males and 21 percent of the females.

Unfortunately, data obtained for humans on this broad subject of organic brain syndrome in the aged is complicated by the past history of the individuals studied. Humans, unlike animals in protected environments, experience numerous insults from the environment. Thus, such factors as mechanical injury (*trauma*) to the head, cancer, infections (such as tertiary *syphilis* or spinal meningitis), extremely high fever, metabolic disorders (such as **hypothyroidism**), and vitamin and **trace element** deficiencies may all add to the otherwise "normal" atrophy of the brain, loss of nerve cells, and atherosclerosis of the cerebral blood vessels. Added to all of this is the possibility of self-intoxication by such injurious substances as alcohol, drugs, and heavy metals like lead and mercury which may be present in the foods we eat. In this connection, it is a sociological truism that people living their lives under low socioeconomic conditions may have more physical illness. They also tend to show a greater incidence of cerebral insults or trauma in the form of head injuries (i.e., from physical encounters like fights, etc.).

Stroke.   Commonly known as **stroke,** the *cerebrovascular accident* is the result of the cutting off of the blood supply to the brain. It is technically referred to as *cerebral infarction.* Eighty percent of strokes are caused by the blockage of an artery to the brain by either the build-up of fatty deposits in the blood vessels (an **atheroma**) or a blood clot (**thrombus**). The remaining 20 percent of cases of stroke are the result of *hemorrhage,* that is, bleeding resulting from a ruptured blood vessel supplying the brain. The end result is an inadequate blood supply to the brain and a reduction in the supply of oxygen and nutrients to cerebral tissues.

The incidence of stroke in the elderly population was investigated over a five-year period (1965–1970) in the Chicago Stroke Study. It was found that the incidence of strokes was higher in the black population than in the white population and that its incidence increased with advancing age in both racial groups. Table 5.1 shows that this is true for both males and females of each race. Thus, during a three-year period of this study over 2.5 times as many black males as white males 65 to 69 years of age suffered strokes, and over 1.5 times as many black females as white females in this group suffered strokes. In the age group 70 to 74 years old, the incidence of strokes among black and white males was much closer, and the figures were essentially identical. However, black females in their seventies still showed approximately 1.5 times as great an incidence of stroke as their white female counterparts (Ostfeld 1976).

To the person concerned with services to the elderly, victims of nonfatal stroke represent a significant part of the older population which requires understanding and often special attention. Although strokes kill many people in the first few hours or days following their onset, not all strokes are fatal. Indeed, some people suffer a number of repeated, minor strokes which may not even require hospitalization. However, in the case of severe strokes, those who survive may require longterm rehabilitation therapy. In many cases, only partial success is achieved in reversing the associated loss in neurological capabilities, especially in regard to mobility and communication. In summary

Table 5.1   The Chicago Stroke Study, 1965–1970

Age	Males		Females	
	White	*Black*	*White*	*Black*
65–69	3.0%	7.8%	4.4%	7.5%
70–74	7.6%	8.9%	8.5%	12.3%

Source: Adapted from Ostfeld 1976.

then, stroke has two major phases: an *acute* phase, when life support may be necessary for survival, and a *chronic* phase, which is usually a longterm period when sometimes only partial recovery of lost function may be achieved. The combined efforts of the geriatric physician, the geriatric practitioner nurse, the geriatric social worker, and the geriatric counselor may be essential whether we are speaking of either of the two phases of cerebral vascular accidents.

Aging of the Autonomic Nervous System

Were one to point to a single general characteristic of *physiological* aging, it would be the increasing relative inability of the body to respond to stress with advancing age. For example, older persons experience increasing difficulty in maintaining the normal body temperature (37° C) when the ambient temperature falls much below 20° C (68° F). In fact, the rectal temperature of humans of advanced age tends to run considerably below 37° C and may often be as low as 32° C (90° F). Likewise, in persons over 60 years of age, there is a much higher mortality rate from heat prostration. Recovery of normal **pulse rate** and respiratory volume following displacement by exercise is progressively reduced with advancing age in people over 65.

In special cases, the failure of certain neuronal elements of the autonomic nervous system may be responsible for the difficulty of senile persons to retain their bowel and bladder contents.

Aging of the Reflexes

A *reflex* or *reflex act* is an involuntary and predictable response of the body to a particular stimulus, which is mediated via the central nervous system. The incoming and outgoing spinal nerves and the spinal cord (with its many nerve tracts) are the pathways for such reflex acts. The specific pathway between the point of stimulation and the responding muscle or gland is the *reflex arc*. In its simplest form, it includes a sensory or *afferent* (receptor) neuron and a motor or *efferent* neuron, arising in the central nervous system. Many reflexes, however, involve more complex pathways, which include one or more intermediate neurons interposed between the sensory and motor neurons.

A stimulus to the ending of a sensory neuron, such as a touch receptor in the skin, results in the initiation of a nerve impulse. The impulse is transmitted either directly or via one or more intermediate (internuncial) neurons to a motor neuron. Excitation of the motor neuron then elicits a reflex

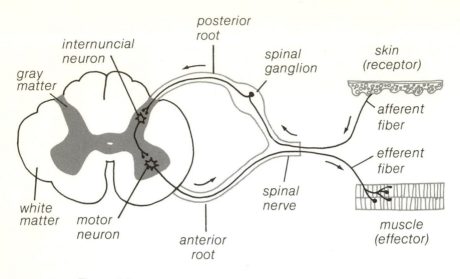

Figure 5.5.   A simple reflex involving a skin receptor, the spinal cord, and skeletal muscle (effector).

response of excitation or inhibition of a muscle or gland (Fig. 5.5). The most common example of a simple reflex is the knee jerk. More complex reflexes include coughing and sneezing and autonomic control of the activities of the heart, the gastrointestinal tract, and the size of the pupil of the eye.

Neurological studies of aged subjects have shown that simple reflex phenomena may be markedly diminished or absent. In one study the *ankle jerk* reflex was found to be absent in 70 percent of the subjects aged 70 to 80. For the same group, the *triceps jerk* was absent in about 20 percent, and the *knee jerk* and *biceps jerk* absent in about 15 percent of the cases. In fact, by the age of 90, an intact jerk reflex was a rare occurrence. Moreover, in some extremely old patients, a particular reflex might be observed on one day and then appear to be absent on the next. However, most of the more deeply seated reflexes appear to be relatively intact up to the age of 60. Thereafter, the ability to produce them becomes progressively less predictable. (See Agate 1963 for details.)

Aging of the Senses

Information about the environment is coded by specialized sensory neurons located on the surface and in internal organs of the body. These sensory receptors transduce (convert) energy changes in the environment (heat, light, sound, vibration, etc.) into nerve impulses which are then transmitted centrally along *afferent* nerves to centers in the cerebrum for processing and perception. Obviously, any decrease in the functional capabilities of these receptors will deprive the organism of valuable information about its environment. The sections which follow describe the known changes which occur in the various senses with age.

Vision

The incidence of blindness from all causes increases with advancing age. In one study, it was shown that less than 0.5 percent of persons 45 to 64 were legally blind (i.e., had less than 20/200 vision in both eyes). On the other hand, approximately 2 percent of people 65 and over fell into this category. In people over 100 years old, 5 percent were blind. In general, blindness sets in late in life. In 11.5 percent of the cases studied, blindness occurred before the age of 45. For 30.7 percent of the total number of cases, blindness set in between the ages of 45 and 64. However, the largest number of cases, 54 percent, occurred in people 65 years of age and over.

Senile changes in the structure of the eye include shrinkage in total mass, increase in the amount of connective (nonvisual) tissue, fatty degeneration, decreased metabolism, **sclerosis,** and reduced blood supply. All these changes lead to a reduction in the functional capabilities of this organ. It should be pointed out that these changes set in much earlier in some individuals than in others.

In persons in their middle forties and older, **presbyopia** is a universally distributed aging phenomenon. Presbyopia, commonly called *farsightedness,* is the inability of the eye to accommodate for close vision. It progresses to a definite, stable end-point within 5 to 10 years. This condition results from an increase in viscosity of the fluid contents of the eye's lens and, therefore, increasing difficulty of the lens to change its shape when focusing over short distances. This condition results in the loss of the capacity to do close work, such as reading or knitting. Thus, young middle-aged persons can reveal their age by having to hold a book or newspaper farther and farther away in order to be able to read it. Fortunately, this condition can be readily remedied with corrective reading glasses. It is interesting to note that progressive presbyopia is said to set in earlier in nonwhites (as early as the age of 40) than in whites.

Other visual changes accompanying presbyopia as a manifestation of aging include a reduction in the size of the visual field perceived and an increased **threshold** to light stimulation. This results in the need for more intense light in order to see well. In addition, adaptation of the eye to darkness, "dark adaptation," commonly slows down after the age of 70. This is due to the increase in the time taken to respond, as well as a corresponding decrease in the *amplitude* of change by the iris (diaphragm) of the eye, in response to light changes.

Cataracts are essentially an opacity of the lens of the eye that develops in many people, mostly after the age of 80. When affecting the major portion of the lens, cataracts severely impair one's vision. However, the use of corrective lenses following surgical removal of the defective lens can partially restore vision in most cases. Finally, the incidence of **glaucoma,** a serious eye condition involving increased intraocular pressure, increases with advancing age. It occurs in 0.5 percent of the population over 40, and it appears to be more marked in women than in men past the ages of 60 to 69. This is especially true when there is a family history of the disease. Failure to recognize and treat glaucoma is one cause of blindness, especially in the elderly.

It is obvious that senile changes in vision tend to limit the activities of an older person. Vision problems may lessen the enjoyment of reading, watching television, and other forms of entertainment. This may cause the older individual to feel even more isolated from society than his or her age status *per se*. In fact, the limitation of activities of a previously active person by defects in vision may trigger depression or more serious psychiatric disorders.

Hearing

In both men and women, hearing sensitivity decreases and the prevalence of *deafness* increases with advancing age. Of individuals 25 to 34 years old, only about 0.5 percent are deaf. The incidence increases to about 1.0 percent in the 35 to 45 age bracket and to about 1.5 percent in 45- to 54-year-olds. Between the ages of 55 and 75, the incidence of deafness rises from about 2.8 percent to well over 15.0 percent. However, the highest incidence of *new* cases of deafness occurs after the age of 65. In contrast to total deafness, the incidence of detectable hearing difficulties rises from 1.6 percent in people 25 to 34 years old to over 27 percent of those over 74.

Hearing loss can occur at virtually any age after birth. Impairment of hearing may be the result of the failure of replacement of auditory neurons in the inner ear as they are lost, due to extremely loud sounds (occupational noise, hard rock music, etc.), disease, or certain drugs. Evidence from cross-sectional studies suggests that there is a gradual, albeit modest, loss in hearing for virtually the entire audible sound spectrum beginning at a very early age up to age 25. Thereafter, hearing loss becomes much more apparent, with the most extreme, severe losses occurring in the ability to hear sounds of higher **pitches.** A 10-year-old child, for example, can hear high-pitched sounds with frequencies of almost 20,000 cycles per second (cps). On the other hand, the upper range of hearing in persons aged 65 is only about 8000 cps. Finally, by age 70, there is at least a 10 decibel loss in hearing at all frequencies.

Discrimination of pitch decreases linearly from 25 to 55 years of age and declines even more rapidly thereafter. The ability to distinguish between two sounds produced in close succession is called *two-click discrimination*. It is a measure of *temporal* discrimination which tends to become more difficult for older people. It has been generally observed that the earlier in life a decline in hearing capacities begins, the more rapid is its progress with advancing age.

Another hearing difficulty, **tinnitus,** is essentially "biological noise" which is actually generated within the auditory system. It is characterized by ringing in the ears. In young persons aged 18 to 24, only 3 percent complain of severe tinnitus; about 9 percent of people aged 55 to 64 experience this affliction. About 11 percent of persons 65 to 74 years of age complain of tinnitus. There is good evidence that this condition is generally more common in women than in men.

Thus, the prevalent functional abnormalities in hearing include reduced sound sensitivity, impaired sound localization, reduced sound discrimination (including *speech* discrimination), disturbed loudness perception, and tinnitus. (For a thorough discussion of the anatomical and physiological factors which underlie these observed changes in hearing, see Weiss 1959.)

Hearing aids are nothing more than electrical amplifiers of sound which may or may not correct any particular hearing impairment. Indeed, in face to face conversation, lip reading is considered very important to persons with hearing disabilities, who learn to do so empirically. This means of communication will, of course, be difficult or impossible for an older person who is likely to be suffering from visual impairments as well. People with hearing problems are often unable to judge how loudly they themselves are speaking and may therefore tend to shout without realizing it. Furthermore, there is a tendency for the pitch of the voice to increase with advancing age. At the same time, speech may also become slurred and articulation may deteriorate, since these people no longer hear clearly what they are saying.

A decrease in hearing sensitivity in the aged often limits the enjoyment of social gatherings, and such entertainment activities as radio, television, and concerts. Hearing loss may also limit or adversely affect more intimate social relationships. Indeed, hearing loss may isolate the older person from the rest of society to such a degree that it may be a potential cause of mild **paranoia.** This would understandably derive from a growing suspicion of others whose conversation they cannot hear or understand. Accordingly, personality and behavior can be dually affected in otherwise normal elderly persons, i.e., both by increasing difficulty in communication and through decreasing social acceptability by such a sensory decrement.

Taste

Based on only scanty evidence, the ability to taste certain chemical substances is said to decline with advancing age. In tests on persons of various ages (Birren 1959), it was found that the ability to taste sugars decreased in older persons. The most marked decrease (as measured by increasing taste threshold) occurred in people aged 52 to 85. On the other hand, this particular study also found that the ability to perceive salty tastes decreases with age in men but not in women.

This loss of taste perception, also reported in subjective accounts by older women and men, is related anatomically to the known diminution in the number of **taste buds** in later life. The number of taste buds is fairly constant through adolescence, but in maturity and into early old age (up to the age of 70), there is a slight decrease in the number of these taste receptors. In advanced old age, however, the number of taste buds is drastically reduced. In a comparison between children and elderly adults (aged 74 to 85) one type of taste bud was found to have declined in number by two-thirds in the elderly group (248 in children to 88 in adults) (Birren 1959). Other factors which contribute to the reduction in taste sensation are the lower secretion of saliva and the fissuring and furrowing of the tongue known to occur in older persons. The loss of taste sensibility probably explains the increased use of condiments or spices observed in the elderly. At the same time, the diminished sense of taste is one of several causes for the loss of appetite which can result in malnutrition, a significant health problem in the elderly, discussed in Chapter 10.

Smell

Data on age-related changes as regards the perception of odors *(olfaction)* are sparse and, unfortunately, contradictory in some cases. In general, it can be said that the sense of smell becomes best developed at puberty and appears to begin to decrease only after the age of 45, continuing to decline gradually thereafter. Microscopic examination of tissue from the lining of the nasal epithelium of people over age 70 shows pronounced atrophy of the **olfactory bulbs.** This is accompanied by a reduction in the number of olfactory nervous elements. It has been estimated that there is an 8 percent loss of olfactory fibers from birth to age 15. Surprisingly, from 76 to 91 years of age, the total loss in such fiber amounts to 73 percent. However, such summary figures are deceptive because the rate of loss of such fibers averages only 0.9 percent per year up to age 37, rising to 1.6 percent per year between ages 37 and 52. Thereafter, however, the rate of loss actually decreases to 0.7 percent per year from ages 52 to 67 to as low as 0.3 percent per year from ages 67 to 82. In general, then, it is accepted that the loss in olfaction with advancing age is related to this cumulative loss in the number of nerve endings in the olfactory nasal epithelium.

In regard to food, the sense of smell contributes almost as much as the sensation arising from the taste buds to the "taste," and, therefore, the attractiveness, of food. Accordingly, the effects of diminished olfactory function with age are very much the same as those of a diminished sense of taste. In addition, a hazardous result of the loss in olfactory sensitivity in very old persons is the inability to detect the odor of dangerous gases (such as illuminating gas) and smoke from fires.

Touch and Pain

Touch sensitivity decreases through the sixth decade of life. This is probably due to the decrease with age in the number and sensitivity of the neuronal receptors on the skin. In the seventh and eighth decades, the trend seems to be reversed and touch sensitivity appears actually to increase, perhaps due to an increasing thinning of the skin with age.

Sensitivity to pain at various ages has also been studied. Sensitivity to such painful stimuli as heat or being rubbed with a rough cloth was found to remain essentially unchanged into old age. However, both empirically and clinically, it has been shown that there is a *decrease* in the sensitivity to such stimuli as a pin prick with advancing age. This may be associated with the changes in the sensory receptors mentioned above. Especially in extremely old individuals, the loss of the sense of touch and pain may have serious consequences because conditions such as dermatitis, cuts, burns, and infection may not be perceived and therefore not be treated.

Summary

Anatomically, there is a progressive loss, with advancing age, in the total number of nerve cells. This is particularly well documented for certain areas of the brain and for senses like vision, hearing, touch, taste, and smell. The *conduction* of nerve impulses along nerve fibers is reduced only slightly. However, impulse *transmission* between two or more neurons *is* slowed significantly in old persons so that reflex responses are slower and weaker. These changes at the cellular level are accompanied by a general decline in the effectiveness of the nervous system to perform its normal regulatory function. The reduced capability of the nervous system to make effective responses to stress in the environment is especially evident. For example, there is a slowing down of protective reflexes, such as the knee jerk and withdrawal reflexes, an increasing difficulty in maintaining normal body temperature with external changes, and a slower recovery from increases in pulse rate and respiratory volume by exercise.

There is a wide variability in changes in cognitive functions such as verbal learning ability, abstract thinking, and storage of new information, especially in persons over 65 years of age. This is in part related to the earlier life style and educational and cultural background of each person. On the other hand, the ability to learn new psychomotor skills is significantly reduced. Short-term memory loss may occur, usually in persons over 75, but it is generally associated with some form of organic brain disease.

Each of the five senses shows a progressive decline in sensitivity to varying degrees. Presbyopia (farsightedness) is a universally distributed aging phenomenon in humans, occurring during the fourth or early fifth decades of life. Failing vision and progressive hearing loss, inevitable concomitants of aging, may adversely affect physical and mental well-being in the older person through their negative social consequences. Lowered sensitivity to pain may reduce the older person's awareness of cuts, burns, and infection, resulting in a neglect of treatment. Finally, a diminished sense of taste and smell in advanced age may affect one's physical health as the desire for food decreases.

References

Agate, J. 1963. The practice of geriatrics. Charles C. Thomas, Springfield, Ill., pp. 280–310.

Birren, J. E., ed. 1959. Handbook of aging and the individual. University of Chicago Press, Chicago. 939 pp.

Birren, J. E., and K. W. Schaie, eds. 1977. Handbook of the psychology of aging. Van Nostrand Reinhold, New York. 787 pp.

Brody, H. 1970. Structural changes in the aging nervous system. Pages 9–21 *in* H. T. Blumenthal, ed., Interdisciplinary topics in gerontology, vol. 7. Karger, New York, pp. 9–21.

Brody, H., and N. Vijayashankar. 1977. Anatomical changes in the nervous system. Pages 241–261 *in* C. E. Finch and L. Hayflick, eds., Handbook of the biology of aging. Van Nostrand Reinhold, New York.

Diamond, M. C. 1978. The aging brain: Some enlightening and optimistic results. American Scientist 66:66–71.

Finch, C. E. 1977. Neuroendocrine and autonomic aspects of aging. Pages 262–274 *in* C. E. Finch and L. Hayflick, eds., Handbook of the biology of aging. Van Nostrand Reinhold, New York.

Goldfarb, A. I. 1975. Memory and aging. Pages 149–186 *in* R. Goldman, M. Rockstein, and M. L. Sussman, eds., The physiology and pathology of human aging. Academic Press, New York.

Laird, D. A., and W. J. Breen. Sex and age alterations in taste preferences. J. Amer. Diet. 15:549–50.

Ostfeld, A. M. 1976. Nutritional aspects of stroke, particularly in the elderly. Page 218 *in* M. Rockstein and M. L. Sussman, eds., Nutrition, longevity, and aging. Academic Press, New York.

Rockstein, M., and M. L. Sussman. 1973. Development and aging in the nervous system. Academic Press, New York. 218 pp.

U.S. Dept. of Health, Education and Welfare. 1974. Working with older people. II. Biological, psychological and sociological aspects of aging. HSM 72-6006. Rockville, Md.

Verwoerdt, A. 1976. Clinical geropsychiatry. Williams and Wilkins, Baltimore. 287 pp.

Weiss, A. D. 1959. Sensory function. Pages 503–542 *in* J. E. Birren, ed., Handbook of aging and the individual. University of Chicago Press.

Welford, A. T. 1959. Psychomotor performance. Pages 561–613 *in* J. E. Birren, ed., Handbook of aging and the individual. University of Chicago Press.

Chapter Six

The Cardiovascular System

The age-related functional decline of the heart and blood vessels, which are collectively referred to as the *cardiovascular system,* has been a problem associated with human aging since early times. For example, the writings of the ancient Greeks describe the changes in blood vessels known as *atherosclerosis.* Recent autopsies of Egyptian mummies have revealed that the Egyptians also suffered from the same disease. In the fifteenth century, the talented and versatile Leonardo da Vinci, who, aside from his other accomplishments, was one of our early great anatomists, referred to "veins which by the thickening of their tunics in the old restrict the passage of blood, and by the lack of nourishment destroy the life of the aged without any fever, the old coming to fail little by little in slow death" (Belt 1952). This description of atherosclerosis is, with minor changes in terminology, as accurate today as it was almost 500 years ago.

Cardiovascular diseases, including arteriosclerosis and atherosclerosis, are currently the major causes of death in most socioeconomically advanced nations. In the United States, for example, more deaths are attributed to diseases of the circulatory system than to any other cause, including cancer. About 39 percent of the deaths recorded in 1976 in the United States were due to heart disease *alone,* while fewer than half that number (about 18 percent) were due to malignant cancer. Prior to the age of 45, however, the death rate from cardiovascular disease is negligible. After that age, the rate rises sharply and peaks in the eighth decade of life. In fact, in persons 65 and over, the number of deaths from heart disease is twice as high as deaths from stroke, the next most common cause of death. Together, arteriosclerosis and atherosclerosis, involving both the heart and blood vessels, kill 9320 people per 100,000 (over 9 percent of the population). The third major cause of death, cancer, claims only about 10 percent of this number (i.e., 993 per 100,000, or only about 1 percent of the population).

The high incidence of death from heart disease, however, is only a small part of the true significance of cardiovascular disorders. That is because people who do survive heart attacks may suffer severe physical, economic, social, and psychological effects; these include full or partial physical disability, reductions in social and economic status due to a forced premature retirement, economic attrition due to the costs of medical care, and a disruption of the normal day-to-day family routine.

Cardiovascular Structure and Function

The *blood* bathes all the tissues of the body, supplying them with nutrients and oxygen and removing waste products. Equalization of body temperature is brought about by circulation of blood. Hormones produced by the various glands are released into the circulation and transported to their target tissues. Antibodies in the blood fight infections everywhere in the body.

The *heart* is a truly remarkable muscular organ. Whereas skeletal muscle requires rest after doing work, cardiac muscle works constantly for as long as the individual lives, resting only a fraction of a second between successive beats. Thus, in an average lifetime of 75 years, the heart may beat 3 billion times without any extended rest. As a powerful pump, the heart expels, when the body is at rest, 4 to 5 liters per minute, or about 75 gallons of blood (240 to 300 liters) each hour. With moderate physical activity, this *cardiac output* doubles and with very strenuous activity it may increase as much as 10 times (i.e., to 700 to 750 gallons of blood per hour). Thus, in a 70-year lifetime, as much as 900 million gallons of blood may be pumped by the average human heart.

The human heart contains four chambers. The two upper chambers are the right and left **atria** (or *auricles*), and the two lower, more muscular chambers are the right and left **ventricles** (Fig. 6.1). Blood from the systemic circulation in all parts of the body returns to the heart via the largest *caval veins* (also called the anterior and posterior vena cava), which empty into the right atrium (Fig. 6.2). This blood is relatively low in oxygen and high in carbon dioxide. Blood is then pumped out by the contraction of the right atrium downward into the right ventricle which, in turn, expels the blood into the **pulmonary** *artery* which supplies the lungs. In the lungs, the blood takes up oxygen and gives off carbon dioxide. Now rich in oxygen, the blood is returned to the left atrium of the heart via the *pulmonary veins*. From this chamber, the blood is propelled into the left ventricle which pumps the blood through the largest artery in the body, the *aorta*. Thence, blood is circulated via the smaller arteries throughout the body (once more in the systemic circulation). **Valves** are located in the heart between each atrium and its corres-

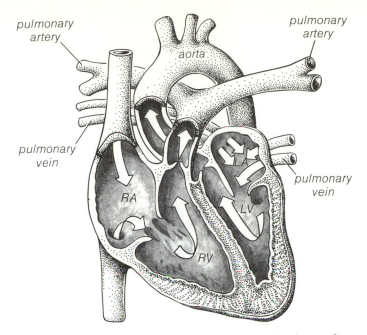

Figure 6.1.   The pathway of blood through the heart of a mammal. RA, right atrium; LA, left atrium; RV, right ventricle; LV, left ventricle. (From Kormondy et al.)

ponding ventricle, between the pulmonary artery and the left atrium, and between the left ventricle and the aorta. These valves serve to prevent the reversal of the flow of blood as each chamber involved contracts.

Blood pressure during the **cardiac cycle** is expressed as the ratio of **systolic** to **diastolic pressure.** The values given refer to the blood pressure during the contraction phase of the cardiac cycle (**systole**) and the blood pressure when the heart's chambers are relaxed and the chambers are filling (**diastole**). Thus the "normal" value of 120/80 for a young adult means that, during *systole,* the pressure which the heart exerts on the blood being expelled can raise a column of mercury (Hg) 120 millimeters (mm.), or about 5 inches, whereas during *diastole,* the pressure so produced measures 80 mm. in height (expressed as 80 mm.Hg).

Aging of the Heart

Anatomical Changes

The gross appearance of the heart shows changes with age. The amount of fat, both in the sac-like lining surrounding the heart, the *pericar-*

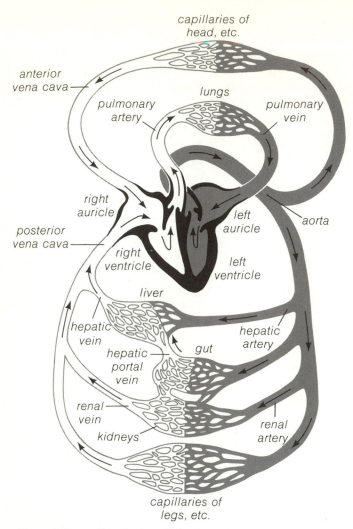

Figure 6.2.   Distribution of blood to major organs of the body. (From Kormondy et al.)

dium, and at the points of entrance of the major cardiac blood vessels, increases. By the fifth decade of life, the fat deposited on the surface of the heart may form a single continuous sheet. The red color of the heart muscle darkens to a deeper brown. **Cardiomegaly** (enlargement of the heart) and **myocardial hypertrophy** (overdevelopment of the heart muscle) are quite common among the elderly. These changes, however, are related to diseases of the heart and blood vessels, including diseases of the heart valves, coronary insufficiency, anemia, or high blood pressure, and cannot be considered part of the normal aging process. In fact, the *size* of the heart in old persons without clinical heart disease or high blood pressure is the same as in middle age. Indeed, it may even be smaller, due, for the most part, to decreased physical demands upon the heart with reduced physical activity during old age.

With advancing age, the **endocardium** (the internal muscle layer lining the four chambers of the heart) thickens due to deposition of connective tissue rich in collagen. Other endocardial changes include the appearance of whitish patches in regions of high pressure due to thickening and sclerosis of cells in the muscle wall. The right ventricle, which is usually under less pressure than other regions of the heart, is relatively spared from such changes.

The *heart valves* become thicker and more rigid due to sclerosis and **fibrosis** with increased deposits of collagen. Also, with advancing age, the collagen in the *aortic valve* undergoes degeneration. The *fibrosa* of the valve calcifies and accumulates lipids, and adhesions form at the bases of the valve cusps. Similar, but less severe changes occur in the *mitral valve,* which separates the left atrium from the left ventricle. The remaining heart valves, the tricuspid and pulmonary valves, show only minor changes with normal aging. However, the incidence of degenerative calcific valve disease is one of the most common features in the aging heart (on postmortem examination), occurring in up to 37 percent of persons over age 75 (Harris 1970, 1971).

Microscopic anatomical changes include a gradual but marked reduction in number and size of the muscle fibers of the heart. This change occurs because all muscle tissue is *postmitotic,* i.e., it lacks the capability to replace cells as they atrophy and die. The amount of lipochrome pigment (lipofuscin) within the muscle also increases as does the collagen in the endocardium, in the valves, and in the artery walls. An aging phenomenon found to be universal in humans is the calcification of arterial walls which causes the arteries to dilate, lengthen, and become less elastic. The walls of the largest artery, the aorta, also become less elastic with advancing age, which produces a typical increase in systolic blood pressure, but has only a little effect on diastolic pressure.

As noted above, in appearance, the heart muscle undergoes "brown atrophy," which is a reduction in heart weight accompanied by the accumulation of lipofuscin pigment in the muscle fibers. Fibrotic **lesions** occur between the fibers of the heart muscle or may totally replace them. These are similar in appearance to the lesions of *ischemic heart disease* (discussed below). *Senile cardiac amyloidosis,* particularly of the left atrium, occurs with increasing frequency with advancing age, that is, in about one out of eight men (12 percent) over 80 years of age and in about 50 percent of those over 90.

Physiological Changes

Cardiac Output.   The amount of blood pumped out of the heart of a normal young adult with each beat (approximately 50 to 60 milliliters) is called the *stroke volume.* This value diminishes by 0.7 percent per year after maturity (20 years of age). The volume of blood pumped by the heart every minute, the *cardiac output,* is merely the product of the stroke volume and the heart rate (pulse). As mentioned earlier, an average normal adult heart, working at the rate of 70 beats a minute, will pump about 4 to 5 liters of blood every minute. At this rate, all the blood in the body is usually pumped through the heart about once every minute.

Cardiac output decreases linearly at the rate of about 0.7 percent per year. Thus, cardiac output decreases from about 5.0 liters per minute at age 20 to about 3.5 liters per minute by age 75. This decrease is due chiefly to a reduction in the stroke volume or, less commonly, to a decrease in the heart rate.

Since both stroke volume and cardiac output vary according to the body size of the individual, they are more correctly expressed as *stroke index* and *cardiac index.* Stroke index (or stroke volume per unit of body surface area) diminishes by 0.49 percent per year after maturity. Cardiac index (or cardiac output per unit of body surface area) decreases by about 0.79 percent per year.

Heart Rate.   From birth to death, the heart (pulse) rate diminishes gradually. A newborn child has a pulse rate of about 140 beats per minute; by age 3, it decreases to about 100. During adolescence, the rate is about 90 per minute, and a young adult male has a pulse of about 70. In older male subjects, the pulse rate is quite variable; however, there is a distinct general tendency for the pulse frequency to decrease between the ages of 60 and 84.

Electrocardiographic Patterns.   The electrocardiogram (EKG) is a magnified record of very small bioelectrical voltages produced during the cardiac cycle (Fig. 6.3). It is monitored with electrodes placed on the arms and legs. The EKG patterns of older individuals show particular, characteristic differences when compared with those of younger persons (Table 6.1). Minor fibroses in the heart's conduction system, cellular changes with age, and other factors may alter only slightly the characteristic wave patterns on the EKG. However, gross pathological changes in the heart (due to disease and not to normal aging processes) do produce very marked characteristic changes in the EKG.

Response to Stress.   Clinicians have long recognized that, with advancing age, there is a progressive loss of cardiac competence, i.e., the

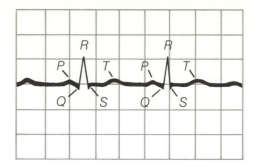

Figure 6.3.   Typical, normal electrocardiogram (EKG).

Table 6.1.   EKG Survey of Residents of Old People's Home

Age group	Normal EKG (percent)	Slightly Abnormal EKG (percent)	Moderately Abnormal EKG (percent)
50–59	58.8	25.9	15.5
60–69	29.3	56.0	14.7
70–79	26.0	58.8	15.4

Source: Adapted from Harris, 1961.

ability of the heart to meet the body's requirements under stressful conditions such as strenuous exercise. For example, the normal heart of a young adult can increase its output four times under stress; whereas the heart of a trained athlete can increase its output six times under similar conditions. The maximum percentage that the cardiac output can increase above normal is called the *cardiac reserve.* Factors which reduce cardiac reserve include **is-chemic heart disease** (decreased oxygen supply to heart cells), valvular disease, and coronary thromboses. Thus, the most common observation in the aging heart is that cardiac reserve diminishes and is unable to increase its output when confronted with sudden or prolonged stress.

Previous physical conditioning and medical history also influence the effectiveness of heart function in later years. Among the elderly who were athletes (long-distance runners, cross-country skiers, etc.), physiological variables which contribute to cardiac reserve were better than those of nonathletic (control) individuals of the same age. For example, maximum oxygen uptake capacity was 42.5 milliliters per kilogram (ml./kg.) of body weight for athletes and 37.1 ml./kg. for the controls. Heart volume was 485 milliliters per square meter (ml./M^2) of body surface among former athletes and 421 ml./M^2 in nonathletes.

Insults to the heart muscle from diseases in youth may cause permanent structural damage which, under conditions of reduced cardiac reserve in later years, may cause the heart to fail under stress. A prime example is rheumatic fever, which, if incurred during youth, may damage the heart valves, so that in later years the damaged heart valves may malfunction, greatly reducing the pumping capacity of the heart. At present, older people suffering from this condition may have such defective heart valves replaced surgically with artificial ones.

Finally, cases of *heart failure* (i.e., the reduction of the pumping capacity of the heart below the level required for the body to function) have been found to develop in older people who have had *no* previous history of coronary disease, high blood pressure, or valvular disease. These cases may represent examples of myocardial (heart muscle) failure due to "normal" aging alone.

The maximum blood flow through the *coronary arteries,* the vessels which nourish the heart muscle itself, decreases by age 60 to about 35 percent of what it was at age 20. Coupled with this reduced blood flow to the heart muscle cells is a reduced capacity for these cells to utilize oxygen. These are two important contributory factors in the increased incidence of heart attacks in the elderly.

Pathological Changes: Heart Disease

Heart disease plays quite a significant part in the lives of many older people. At the beginning of this chapter, we stressed the importance of heart disease as the principal cause of death among the elderly. Moreover, heart disease as a *chronic* condition is a common feature among the elderly population. In one study, it was estimated that 40 percent of the elderly living at home had definite evidence of heart disease; in the age group 75 and over, 50 percent were so affected (Caird and Dall 1973). Among older people with minor disabilities, 22 percent had clinical evidence of heart disease which contributed, at least in part, to their disability. A study of the admissions to the geriatric unit of one hospital showed that about 14 percent of the patients were admitted for *congestive heart failure,* a condition in which the heart has diminished cardiac output and contractility, leading to increased heart size, increased venous pressure, and the collection of fluid, or **edema,** throughout the body, particularly in the lungs, liver, and legs. Thus, *heart failure* is the reduction in the functional capacities of the heart (from any cause) below those required by the body, whereas *congestive heart failure* involves the more gradual increase in venous pressure with a build-up of fluid congestion in other organs of the body. Other important types of heart disease among the elderly include **cardiac arrhythmias,** *ischemic heart disease,* and hypertensive heart disease.

Cardiac arrhythmias are irregularities in the normal sequence of heartbeats. Occasional additional heartbeats (termed **ectopic beats**) may be produced by irregular (out of sequence) contractions of the atria or ventricles. Arrhythmias are evident in the electrocardiograms of approximately 40 percent of healthy individuals. The frequent occurrence of ectopic beats is less common. Other common arrhythmias such as ventricular **tachycardia** (the overly rapid contraction of the ventricles) and atrial **flutter** and **fibrillation** (irregular contraction of the atria) are also more common among the elderly. The most common of these conditions, atrial fibrillation, occurs in about 3 to 5 percent of the older population living at home. Cardiac arrhythmias are dangerous when they alter the normal cycle of contraction of the heart. Rapid and irregular contractions of one region of the heart may cause the improper filling of the chamber (or chambers) involved, which may in turn lead to a reduced pumping capacity (cardiac output) of the entire heart. The coronary arteries of a rapidly beating heart (tachycardia) may be unable to nourish the cells of the heart muscle, leading to conditions of *ischemia*.

Ischemic heart disease occurs when the cells of the heart muscle do not receive adequate amounts of oxygen. This condition is the most important heart disease among the elderly, occurring in about 12 percent of women and 20 percent of men over the age of 65. It is a primary contributory cause of heart failure among the elderly. The incidence of ischemic heart disease shows a steady increase with advancing age.

Hypertensive heart disease is characterized by a blood pressure higher than 180/110 (**hypertension**), accompanied by left ventricular hypertrophy (enlargement). This condition occurs in 16 percent of women and 8 percent of men aged 65 to 74. Among persons over the age of 75, the incidence is 12 percent for women and 13 percent for men.

Aging of the Systemic Circulation

As has been indicated earlier, blood is pumped by the heart to all regions of the body through a series of blood vessels, the arteries. The blood leaves the left ventricle via the aorta and flows to the tissues of the body, through arterial branches of ever-decreasing diameter, the smallest of which are the *arterioles;* these empty into the capillary circulation of each organ or tissue. The *venous system* collects blood from the capillaries, beginning with the smallest veins, the *venules.* It returns blood to the heart through vessels of progressively increasing diameter, terminating in the largest veins, the caval veins, which enter the heart. The capillaries connect the arteries and veins in the tissues (Fig. 6.4). The capillaries are tubes of such small diameter that

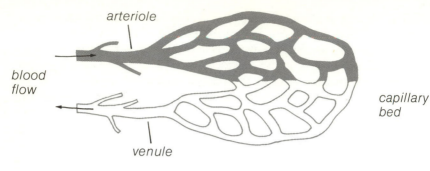

arteriole

blood
flow

venule

capillary
bed

Figure 6.4.   A typical capillary bed.

blood cells may have to pass singly, one by one, through their narrow internal diameter. It is through the thin walls of the capillaries that the oxygen, carbon dioxide, and wastes are exchanged in the tissues.

Structural Changes

The most prevalent form of structural change in the *arteries* is *arteriosclerosis,* a term for any degenerative vascular change leading to the progressive thickening and loss of resiliency of the arterial wall. *Atherosclerosis* is a specific type of vascular alteration that involves the deposit of *atheromas,* or fatty plaques, that accumulate in the arterial wall. Atherosclerosis is a widely distributed disease, occurring in many animal species. All human beings, if they live long enough, will have some degree of atherosclerosis. This condition may begin in early childhood and continue to worsen progressively until it gradually destroys the arteries. Since atherosclerosis damages the major blood vessels, including the aorta and the cerebral and coronary arteries, the heart, brain, and other vital organs are deprived of oxygen and other nutrients. Thus atherosclerosis contributes to ischemic heart disease, cerebrovascular disorders, and abnormal mental states. When arterial walls become weak, the vessels may balloon (a condition called an **aneurysm**) and may even rupture.

With advancing age, cell proliferation and connective tissue formation cause structural changes in the artery wall. Increased mineralization may also occur. During human growth, the elastin content of the arterial wall layers decreases and collagen levels increase. (**Elastin,** a protein, is a principal constituent of elastic tissue.) However, among the elderly, this pattern is reversed. The outer arterial layer calcifies progressively. The degree of calcification is highest in those vessels with high elastin levels, where the mineral appears to be bound to elastin. With advancing age, elastin appears to be able to bind more calcium. Calcification of elastin results in increased loss of elasticity of the arterial walls. At age 25, the calcium content of human aortic elastin is about 1 percent; it is 4 percent at age 65.

Many of the changes associated with aging in the arteries also occur in the smallest vessels of the arterial tree. Throughout life, there is a gradual **involution** (degradative change) of all small arteries and a thickening of the arteriole walls so that the diameter of the blood passageways is reduced in some regions. Changes in shape of the smallest arteries may also occur.

Veins have not been studied as extensively as arteries. Although it is believed that changes occur similar to those reported for arteries, because of the relatively lower blood pressures in these vessels, such changes occur to a lesser degree.

Functional Changes

Blood pressure depends on cardiac output, the elasticity of the arteries, and peripheral resistance. Thus a *decrease* in blood pressure would be expected to result from a reduced cardiac stroke volume and increased volume of the distended aorta with advancing age. However, the increasing stiffness of the walls of the blood vessels and increasing resistance of the "peripheral" vessels to blood flow with age actually results in an *increase* in blood pressure. Thus blood pressure is the result of several interacting factors, and changes with age reflect a composite of changes in these several factors (Table 6.2).

Cross-sectional studies of many different populations indicate that systolic blood pressure generally increases with age, together with a slower rise in the diastolic pressure. However, after age 75, blood pressure does not tend to rise and may even decline. This statistic may be misleading, however,

Table 6.2   Mean Blood Pressure in Adults by Age and Sex, 1960–1962 (mm.Hg)

Age	Men		Women	
	Systolic	Diastolic	Systolic	Diastolic
18–24	121	72	112	69
25–34	125	76	116	73
35–44	129	81	123	78
45–54	134	83	134	82
55–64	140	83	147	85
65–74	148	81	160	84
75–79	154	79	157	79

Source: From the National Center for Health Statistics, 1964.

since many individuals suffering from high blood pressure die before reaching that age, leaving only those people with lower blood pressures in the older population sample.

Summary

The progressive and physiologically irreversible changes associated with the aging of the cardiovascular system include the following: (1) diminished capability of the heart rate to compensate in response to stress; (2) decreased efficiency of the heart as a pump, as evidenced by reduced cardiac output; (3) hardening of the arteries (arteriosclerosis); (4) reduced elasticity of blood vessel walls due to altered elastin; (5) increased peripheral vascular resistance; and (6) increased blood pressure. While atherosclerosis and hypertension appear to be related to the normal aging process, their development may be complicated by such important factors as diet and life style.

References

Agate, J. 1963. The practice of geriatrics. Charles C. Thomas, Springfield, Ill., pp. 162–243.

Belt, E. 1952. Leonardo da Vinci's study of the aging process. Geriatrics 7:205–210.

Caird, F. I., and J. L. C. Dall. 1973. The cardiovascular system. Pages 122–160 *in* J. C. Brocklehurst, ed., Textbook of geriatric medicine and gerontology. Churchill Livingstone, Edinburgh and London.

Harris, R. 1961. The heart in old age. Pages 22–30 *in* Cardiology: An encyclopedia of the cardiovascular system, vol. 5. McGraw-Hill, New York.

Harris, R. 1970. The management of geriatric cardiovascular disease. J. B. Lippincott, Philadelphia. 306 pp.

Harris, R. 1971. Special features of heart disease in the elderly patients. Pages 81–102 *in* A. B. Chinn, ed., Working with older people. U.S. Dept. of Health, Education and Welfare, Rockville, Md.

Harris, R. 1975. Cardiac changes with age. Pages 109–122 *in* R. Goldman, M. Rockstein, and M. Sussman, eds., The physiology and pathology of human aging. Academic Press, New York.

Kohn, R. R. 1977. Heart and cardiovascular system. Pages 281–312 *in* C. E. Finch and L. Hayflick, eds., Handbook of the biology of aging. Van Nostrand Reinhold, New York.

Taylor, H. L., and H. J. Montoye. 1972. Physical fitness, cardiovascular function and age. Pages 223–241 *in* A. M. Ostfield and D. C. Gibson, eds., Epidemiology of aging. U.S. Dept. of Health, Education and Welfare, Bethesda, Md.

Timiras, P. S. 1972. Developmental physiology and aging. Macmillan, New York, pp. 477–501.

Chapter Seven

The Respiratory System

Particularly in the case of the lungs and their associated airways passages, it is difficult to distinguish between (1) pathological changes due to the cumulative effects of environmental trauma, with advancing age, and (2) "true" biological aging processes characterized by *involutionary* structural and concomitant functional changes, especially the reduced capability to deal with stress. Of all the organ systems showing deteriorative changes with advancing age, the respiratory system suffers most from continuous environmental assault and insults, such as air pollution, smoking, and not infrequent respiratory infections. In this connection, "normal" aging changes are diffuse and more or less uniformly distributed throughout the entire lung. On the other hand, pathological changes are generally nonuniform and destructive, occurring in limited, often specific regions of the lung. Because quantitative pulmonary function tests can be readily made on human subjects without sedation or "invasion" and with little if any physical discomfort, extensive data on age changes in respiratory function are readily obtained and available for persons of all ages.

In this chapter, after reviewing the structure and functions of the respiratory system and the measurements of lung capacity in the normal young adult, the changes found in the structure of the rib cage and the airways and lungs in normal elderly people will be discussed. Measurements of respiratory capacity and effectiveness in the older adult are compared to those in the younger adult. Finally, diseases of the respiratory system most prevalent in the elderly are described, with reference to the contribution of such factors as air pollution and smoking to these disease processes.

Anatomy

The respiratory system includes the lungs and its associated air passageways (Fig. 7.1). Air enters through the nose and mouth and passes

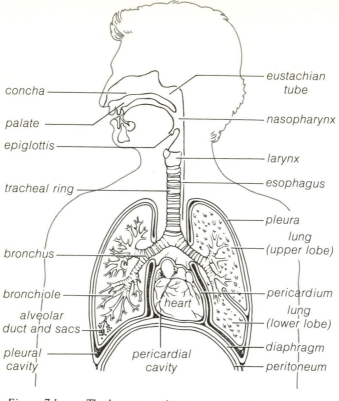

concha

palate

epiglottis

tracheal ring

bronchus

bronchiole

alveolar
duct and sacs

pleural
cavity

eustachian
tube

nasopharynx

larynx

esophagus

pleura

lung
(upper lobe)

pericardium

lung
(lower lobe)

diaphragm

peritoneum

heart

pericardial
cavity

Figure 7.1.   The human respiratory system. (From Kormondy
et al.)

into the **pharynx,** a common chamber for the respiratory passageways and the
gastrointestinal tract (see Chapter 8). From the pharynx, air enters the voice
box, the **larynx,** and then enters the **trachea,** or windpipe, which is held rigid
by C-shaped rings of **cartilage.** The inner, moist epithelium that lines the
trachea is endowed with microscopic, hair-like processes, called **cilia,** which
are capable of moving mucus and foreign particles outward. The trachea
subdivides into a right and a left **bronchus,** each similar in structure to the
trachea. The *bronchi* subdivide into the **bronchioles,** tubes of progressively
smaller diameter richly endowed with **smooth muscle,** each containing only
several small bar-shaped cartilages. The bronchioles lead, by way of alveolar
ducts, into millions of thin-walled air sacs called **alveoli** (Fig. 7.2). An
alveolus is a hollow, sac-like structure formed of extremely thin epithelial
cells. Lying between the outer sides of adjacent clusters of alveoli is found a
richly distributed supply of capillaries, arising from branches of the left and
right pulmonary arteries. These alveoli so richly endowed with surrounding
capillaries, together with supportive connective tissue, make up the lungs.

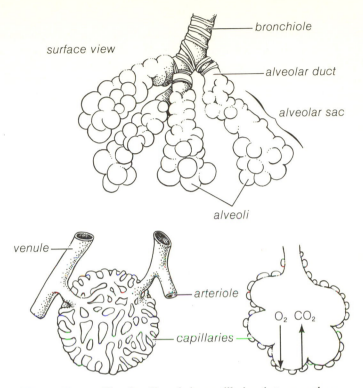

Figure 7.2.   The alveoli and the capillaries that cover them.
(From Kormondy et al.)

The lungs are enclosed in the chest cage, which is formed by the ribs, which are connected by *cartilage* to the breastbone (the *sternum*), in front, and to the vertebrae of the spinal column in the back. The **diaphragm,** a dome-shaped sheet of connective tissue and muscle (see Fig. 7.1), serves as the lower boundary of the *thoracic cavity,* which houses the lungs and heart. The diaphragm separates the thoracic cavity from the lower abdominal cavity. Each lung is enclosed in a doubled layer sac, the *pleura,* each layer being separated from the other by a thin film of fluid (Fig. 7.1).

Physiology

Respiration in broad terms involves both exchange of oxygen and **carbon dioxide** between the outside air and (the air sacs of) the lungs *(ventilation* or *external* respiration) as well as between the blood supply and all cells of the body *(internal* respiration). This chapter will be limited, however, to a discussion only of aging of the lungs and associated airway structures, and, therefore, to functional senescence of ventilation or external respiration.

Venous blood, rich in carbon dioxide and poor in oxygen, returns from all cells of the body to exchange carbon dioxide for oxygen in the alveoli. Through the process of ventilation, the carbon dioxide is transferred from the alveoli to the outside air while oxygen passes into the alveoli. Ventilation consists of two phases, **inspiration** (inhalation) and **expiration** (exhalation). During inspiration the *intercostal* muscles that separate the ribs and the dome-shaped diaphragm both contract. The elevation of the ribs upward and outward and the more horizontal *placement* of the diaphragm causes the total size of the thoracic (chest) cavity to increase. This increase in volume produces a decrease in pressure within the lungs (intrapulmonary pressure) resulting in a weak vacuum which pulls air into the air sacs from the exterior. Expiration is a more passive process, the chest cage falling due to the weight of the ribs and the relaxation of their supporting intercostal muscles. Expiration is accompanied by a contraction of the muscles in the abdominal wall as the diaphragm relaxes, which enhances the increasing intrapulmonary as well as intra-alveolar pressure and results in the expulsion of air from the alveoli to the outside.

Lung Volumes

To appreciate the details of aging of respiratory function, some knowledge of the various measurable volumes of the lungs is necessary. **Tidal volume** is the amount of air moving into and out of the lungs during one cycle of quiet respiration, which is approximately 450 to 500 milliliters (ml.) in a normal young adult male. **Respiratory minute volume** is the volume of air exchanged during normal breathing *per minute*. For a normal male with a tidal volume of 500 ml. breathing at the average rate of 12 times per minute, the *respiratory minute volume* (or *pulmonary ventilation*) is 12 x 500, or approximately 6000 ml. (6 liters) per minute.

Vital capacity, about 4 to 5 liters for normal adult males, is the amount of air which a person can inhale and exhale by a single, forced, maximal inspiration followed by a forcible expiration. This value may be as low as 3.5 liters in sedentary males and as high as 6.5 liters in trained male athletes. *Residual volume* is the amount of unexchanged air that remains in the lungs following a complete, forced expiration. It is reciprocally related to the vital capacity and, accordingly, a measure of age-related *ventilating effectiveness,* particularly under stress. It is a little greater than 1 liter in normal young adult males and slightly lower in young adult females.

Of greater clinical significance is the maximum amount of air which the body is able to move in and out of the lungs by forced voluntary breathing *in a given period of time*—the *maximum breathing capacity*. This *timed* lung volume is essentially a reflection of the degree of **compliance** of the lungs. *Compliance* is a measurement of the ability of the thoracic cage and the lungs to expand as the intrapulmonary pressure decreases during inspiration. It is a measure of both the elastic resistance or stiffness of the rib cage, in relation to the elasticity of the intercostal muscles and flexibility of the rib cartilage, and of the distensibility of the air passageways and the alveoli themselves.

Normal Aging of the Respiratory System

Aside from the effects of air pollutants, noxious gases, smoking, radiation, and respiratory disease, a number of characteristic age-related changes in the respiratory system occur in virtually all persons with advancing age.

Anatomical Changes

The Rib Cage and Pleural Cavity.   **Kyphosis,** the forward curvature of the spine, is a fairly common occurrence in older persons. If not due to a lifelong stooping posture, it may result from a progressive weakening of certain muscles of the neck and back as one grows older. The cartilage connecting the ribs to the spinal column and the sternum show progressive calcification and, therefore, stiffening with age. This reduced expandability of the rib cage, accompanied by a diminution in the number and size of the muscle fibers (see Chapter 11) of the intercostal muscles and of the diaphragm, diminishes contraction effectiveness. The net effect of all of these structural changes is an increasing rigidity, with age, of the rib cage and, therefore, a progressive decrease in compliance. Indeed, it has been shown that there is a steady decrease in chest wall compliance from *birth* through *old age*.

The Airways.   Similarly, the trachea and bronchi become increasingly rigid with the passage of time, due to progressive calcification of their cartilage. The bronchioles are also rendered less distensible by the progressive replacement, with non-contractile tissue, of the decreasing numbers of smooth muscle fibers in the bronchiolar walls. Together with changes in the rib cage compliance, the result is a sizeable decrease of 55 to 60 percent in *maximum breathing capacity* from 25 to 85 years of age (see Table 7.1) in persons otherwise essentially free of respiratory disease. This aging of respiratory function may be aggravated by **emphysema,** a disease of the lungs most prevalent in later life (discussed below).

Microscopically, the epithelial cells lining the trachea and bronchi as well as the cells' ciliary processes show a progressive atrophy (degeneration) with age. This condition is especially severe in smokers and in residents of regions with a high level of air pollution. The glands of these tubes also undergo progressive degeneration. The resulting, increasingly viscous mucus which they secrete becomes more difficult to raise and less effective in protecting against any noxious foreign particles (including bacteria) inhaled in the air.

The Lungs.   The lungs decrease in weight with age. Their color changes gradually from yellowish-pink to gray, with patches of black (chiefly from carbon particles in the air) increasing in number with age. The alveoli, numbering about 24 million at birth, increase to about 300 million at maturity and then remain undiminished in number throughout life. However, the walls separating adjacent alveoli, the alveolar **septa,** do show progressive destruction with time. The net result is a decrease in total *functional respiratory surface* of the lungs by 0.27 square meters (about 2.9 square feet) per year from young adult to old age. At the same time, at the microscopic level, the adult alveolus shows a decrease with time in the *collagen* in relation to the *elastin* content of the alveolar walls. Since the total resiliency and elasticity of these air sacs is due more to the collagen than elastin fibers, as the ratio of collagen to elastin falls so does the ability of the air sacs to expand on inspiration, with advancing age (Klocke 1977).

Likewise, complex changes with age in the chemical components of the substances filling the spaces between the alveoli and the capillaries, called "ground substances," tend to reduce the effectiveness of gas exchange between the interior of the air sacs and their blood supply.

Blood Vessels.   The elasticity of the walls of the pulmonary arteries to the lungs decreases considerably more slowly than the elasticity of the aorta. However, the capillaries supplying the alveoli of the lungs *do* undergo degenerative changes with age similar to those of most other organs of the body (see Chapter 6).

Functional Changes

Rate of Respiration.   The average normal adult shows little change with age in the rate of respiration, which is about 12 to 14 breaths per minute well into old age (Table 7.1). However, it is not unusual in the very old for *expiratory* effort to become more pronounced than *inspiratory* activity. *Periodic (Cheynes-Stokes) breathing,* characterized by forced deep breaths

Table 7.1   Mean Values and Standard Deviations of the Distribution of Individual Values for Minute Ventilation, Breathing Rate, Vital Capacity and Maximum
Breathing Capacity by Age Decade Groups

Age Group*	Minute Volume (L./min.)	Breathing Rate (breaths/min.)	Vital Capacity (L.)	Breathing Capacity (L./min.)
20–29 yr.	5.92	13.1	5.65	165.7
n = 13	± .83	± .8	± .84	± 32.6
30–39 yr.	6.21	14.7	4.96	146.7
n = 70	±1.00	± 2.5	±1.18	± 29.4
40–49 yr.	6.31	14.6	4.82	139.1
n = 100	±1.09	± 2.8	± .77	± 30.0
50–59 yr.	6.21	14.6	4.49	127.8
n = 93	± .88	± 2.5	± .70	± 26.2
60–69 yr.	6.27	14.2	4.18	117.3
n = 71	±1.25	± 1.2	± .79	± 27.3
70–79 yr.	6.22	14.4	3.87	106.2
n = 55	± .89	± 2.3	± .67	± 30.9
80–89 yr.	5.91	13.2	3.38	75.5
n = 8	±2.63	± .6	± .68	± 32.1

*This table includes data from first visit tests only. n, number of persons in decade groups.

Source: Adapted from Norris, Mittman, and Shock 1964.

followed by more shallow breathing, is common in the very old person due to a reduced regularity of nerve impulses from aging nerve centers in the brain and brain stem.

Tidal Volume.   The depth of breathing (about 500 ml. per breath in a young adult male) changes very little through the eighth decade of life. However, tidal volume is not a good index of the *effectiveness* of ventilation, since the nonfunctional portion of the tidal volume, the *dead space volume,* actually increases steadily with advancing age. Thus, the ratio of dead space to tidal volume (about 20 to 25 percent in young healthy adults) falls at a steady rate of 2.4 percent per decade in men and of 1.8 percent per decade in women.

Respiratory Minute Volume.   Since this value is the arithmetical product of the respiratory rate times the tidal volume, it is obvious that this measurement of air movement into and out of the lungs likewise remains constant through very old age (Table 7.1). However, as indicated above, the dead space volume increases steadily with age as the amount of *functional* alveolar volume per breath falls. This means that, at a constant respiratory minute volume, more and more of the air taken in with each breath is functionally less effective with age, as less and less of the tidal air is in contact with functional alveolar epithelial surface. Thus the *efficiency* of gas exchange falls with age, despite the anomalous undiminished *depth, rate,* and *minute volume* of respiration with age.

Vital Capacity.   With the *decreasing* chest cavity compliance and diminished distensibility of the bronchioles related to age, the maximum amount of air which can be taken into the lungs with each breath diminishes markedly (Table 7.1), decreasing by 40 percent from 25 to 85 years of age in both men and women. A decrease in vital capacity results in an increase in the residual air volume, which is especially significant during physically stressful situations such as heavy exercise or other strenuous physical exertion.

Maximum Breathing Capacity.   This measure of the amount of air which a person can exchange with the outside in a 12-second period by forced voluntary breathing falls steadily throughout life from about 33 liters per 12 seconds (or 165 liters per minute) at 25 years of age to less than half that value (75 liters per minute) at age 85 (Table 7.1). This important, clinically valuable diagnostic measurement is an index of altered compliance with age, which indicates, in turn, an increasing inability of the body to adjust its respiratory exchange rate to stress as one grows older.

Pathological Aging of the Respiratory System

As indicated earlier, more than in most other systems, differentiating between normal and pathological aging of the respiratory system is increasingly complicated by the effects of environmental insults such as air pollution, smoking, radiation, and the variety of respiratory infections experienced throughout life, ranging from the common cold to pneumonia. Two of these factors, air pollution and smoking, are particularly linked to pathological aging.

Environmental Factors

Air Pollution.   Longterm exposure to air pollution may be work-related when a person's employment involves exposure to coal, asbestos, nickel, or chromium dust. Similarly, persons living in areas of severe air pollution may be chronically exposed to clouds of noxious gas or suspended particles which stagnate over heavily industrialized areas under appropriate atmospheric conditions. Acute respiratory distress and even death, especially among older persons with cardiopulmonary disease, have been known to result from such conditions.

Exposure to high concentrations of air pollutants destroys the functional epithelial surface of the alveoli and the ciliated surfaces of the larger air passageways. Secondary damage to the capillaries of the alveoli may result, in severe cases, in fluid exudation (acute *chemical* pneumonia). Low concentrations of such pollutants may produce less pronounced, but similar damage to the epithelial surface of the air passages and alveoli. Inflammation of the lining of these structures (chronic *pneumonitis*) with its attendant discomfort results.

Smoking.   Smoking is a unique example of the voluntary pollution of one's own lungs. Statistics have shown repeatedly that smoking is positively correlated with the incidence of cancer of the lung and emphysema. Thus, whereas the occurrence of lung cancer among nonsmokers increases very slowly with advancing age, by contrast, regular cigarette smokers showed a significant increase in the incidence of lung cancer from 50 to 64 years of age (Hammond and Horn 1958). Lung cancer has a 10 to 15 times greater incidence in persons smoking more than 10 cigarettes a day and shows an increasingly greater incidence with advancing age compared to nonsmokers. Figure 7.3 shows that, in a population of 187,783 men under study, the

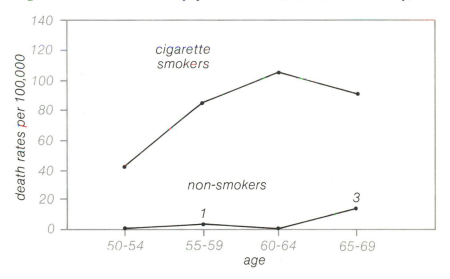

Figure 7.3.   Difference in death rates from lung cancer in male cigarette smokers versus nonsmokers, aged 50–69. (Adapted from Hammond and Horn.)

death rate for lung cancer in nonsmokers showed an increase from 0 to 3 per 100,000 persons, whereas this rate in cigarette smokers increased from 40 to 100 per 100,000 from age 50 to 64.

Pulmonary Diseases

Emphysema.   This is primarily a disease of later life and is definitely related to age. Liebow (1964) has shown that among persons 40 to 50 years old, 24 percent showed *no* sign of emphysema, 30 percent showed *slight* signs, and 30 percent showed *marked* evidence of the disease. Among people aged 90 or over, 64 percent showed *marked* signs and the remaining 36 percent showed *some* signs of this disease. Extreme emphysema is virtually always seen in the later years of longterm heavy smokers.

Emphysema is an age-related, degenerative disorder of the *septa* (walls) separating adjacent alveoli. As the septa are gradually destroyed, they are replaced in part by fibrous tissue (*pulmonary fibrosis*), diminishing the *effective respiratory surface* of the air sacs of the lungs. Consequently, alveolar ventilation decreases while the dead space volume reciprocally increases. At the same time, the elasticity of the bronchioles and alveoli and, therefore, lung distensibility diminishes with the progressive "normal" age-related pulmonary fibrosis. Thus, older persons with extreme cases of emphysema may have a maximum breathing capacity as low as 40 liters per minute in addition to extremely high residual volumes. Any greater-than-normal activity, such as walking stairs, may involve extreme respiratory distress in such persons.

Other Pulmonary Diseases.   Although the common cold, viral or bacterial pneumonia, or (less commonly today) tuberculosis are respiratory diseases not unique to the older person, death from pulmonary infections is most frequent in persons over 65. Bronchial pneumonia especially is often associated with heart failure in older persons (Chapter 6).

Tuberculosis is also more common and more debilitating in persons over 65, especially among economically and socially deprived people including alcoholics and abandoned older persons. Lowered resistance (immunity) with advancing age also makes reinfection from dormant lung abscesses more likely. Similarly, emphysema, diabetes, and other diseases more common among older people may increase the likelihood of tubercular infection in this segment of the population.

Pulmonary emboli, that is, blood clots blocking the circulation in blood vessels of the lung, often prove fatal. They are more likely to occur in older persons who are debilitated or immobilized because of any one of a number of age-related infirmities. The special risk of pulmonary emboli in elderly surgical patients can be minimized by early ambulation following surgery.

Summary

With advancing age, irreversible changes in the structures of the rib cage and of the small air passageways and air sacs of the lungs result in a gradual failure in respiratory compliance. The result is a reduced vital capacity and, more importantly, a diminished capability of moving air into and out of the lungs rapidly, the maximum breathing capacity. The age-related degeneration in the air sacs is accompanied by a reduction in the total functional respiratory surface and, thus, reduced effectiveness of ventilation with each breath taken.

Complicating and aggravating these normal, age-related, involutionary changes of the respiratory system is the lifelong exposure to air pollution especially by people who live in urban industrial areas. Similarly, smoking and the cumulative damage resulting from infectious respiratory diseases tend to exacerbate otherwise normal age-related degenerative changes in the respiratory system. Heavy smoking is particularly linked with the increasing incidence of emphysema and lung cancer in the elderly.

Finally, age-related, lowered immunity to infection, as well as chronic bronchitis of unknown etiology common in older persons, make this age group especially susceptible to viral and bacterial respiratory infection, particularly pneumonia.

References

Cander, L., and J. H. Moyer, eds. 1964. Aging of the lung. Grune and Stratton, New York and London. 371 pp.

Hammond, E. C., and D. Horn. 1958. Smoking and death rates: Report on 44 months of follow-up of 187,783 men. Journal of the American Medical Association 166:1159, 1294.

Klocke, R. A. 1977. Influences of aging on the lung. Pages 432–444 in C. E. Finch and L. E. Hayflick, eds., Handbook of the biology of aging. Van Nostrand Reinhold, New York.

Liebow, A. A. 1964. Biochemical and structural changes in the aging lung: Summary. Pages 97–99 in L. Cander and J. H. Moyer, eds., Aging of the lung. Grune and Stratton, New York and London.

Norris A., C. Mittman, and N. W. Shock. 1964. Lung function in relation to age: Changes in ventilation with age. Page 138 in L. Cander and J. H. Moyer, eds., Aging of the lung. Grune and Stratton, New York and London.

Chapter Eight

The Gastrointestinal System

Since the body receives and digests nutrients through the gastrointestinal system, its functioning is essential to health. In this chapter, we will examine how aging affects the digestive or gastrointestinal system. As a basis for our discussion, the chapter begins with the fundamental structural components of the system and the basic processes of digestion. We will then look at the aging process in the important segments of the digestive tract—the mouth, esophagus, stomach, and intestines—and in the accessory organs of the digestive system—the teeth, salivary glands, the liver, and the gall bladder. How emotional and psychological factors can influence appetite and digestive functions and, therefore, induce or aggravate gastrointestinal disorders in the elderly will also be discussed.

Anatomy and Physiology

The gastrointestinal tract, also called the alimentary canal, is essentially a long, winding tube, beginning with the mouth and ending with the anal opening. Its function is to ingest and digest foods and, finally, to transfer nutrients, minerals, and vitamins into the body's circulation for use by the various cells of the body. It is assisted in these functions by such accessory organs as the teeth and salivary glands, the liver, the gall bladder, and the pancreas. The gastrointestinal tract is subdivided into several segments: the esophagus, the stomach, the small intestine, and the large intestine or **colon** (Fig. 8.1).

The Mouth, Esophagus, and Stomach

In the *mouth,* food is mechanically reduced by chewing and is moistened. Its starch content is partially digested by the mucus and enzyme (**ptyalin**) secreted into the mouth by three pairs of salivary glands. From the

99

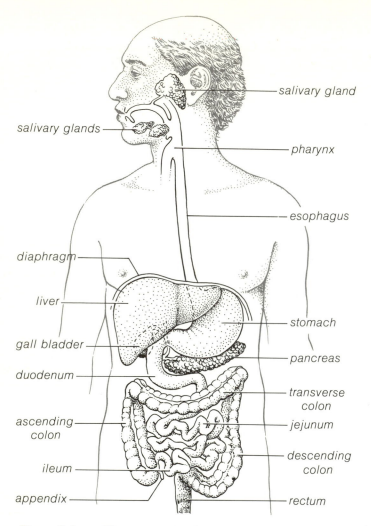

Figure 8.1.   The anatomy of the human digestive system. (From Kormondy et al.)

mouth, the food **bolus** passes through the *pharynx* into the short **esophagus.** The thin wall of the esophagus is lined with circular muscles. The contraction of these muscles (**peristalsis**) moves the food bolus posteriorly past the now open *cardiac* **sphincter,** a valve-like muscular structure, into the *stomach.* As the sphincter closes, the heavily muscularized stomach wall churns and mechanically partly reduces the food bolus. At the same time, the enzyme **pepsin,** which is highly active in the stomach's highly acidic medium, partially digests the proteins in the food.

The Small Intestine

When the mixture of partially digested food and digestive secretions is in a nearly liquid form, this *chyme* passes through the now open *pyloric sphincter* into the *duodenum,* the first and shortest segment of small intestine. A common bile duct from the gall bladder and the pancreatic duct empty their contents into the duodenum. **Bile,** produced in the liver and stored in the gall bladder, emulsifies fats, rendering them more readily digestible by the **lipases** secreted by both the pancreas and the intestine. The lipases reduce the fats to fatty acids and glycerol. In the alkaline medium of the duodenum, partially digested starches and complex sugars are reduced further to simple (monosaccharide) sugars like glucose, fructose, and galactose. Partially digested proteins are further reduced to their elemental components, *amino acids,* by the pancreatic enzyme **trypsin,** and by the various protein-splitting enzymes (proteases) secreted by the lining of the duodenum.

During the ensuing period of digestion in the *jejunum* and *ileum,* the chyme is moved forward and then partially backward in a rhythmic fashion along the 22-foot-long small intestine. Numerous circular folds as well as the **villi,** velvety finger-like outgrowths of the inner wall, line the small intestine (Fig. 8.2). The **microvilli** are additional hair-like projections on the surface of each of the villi. Together, these structures provide a tremendous absorptive surface, equal to 10 square meters (approximately 1100 square feet). Monosaccharides and amino acids are absorbed directly into the capillaries of the villi, and digested fats are absorbed into their centrally located *lacteals* (which empty into the lymph vessels).

The Large Intestine

After four to six hours in the small intestine, the remaining chyme empties into the *colon* through the now open *ileocecal valve* or sphincter. In the colon, water, vitamins, and salts are absorbed. Thus, the chyme is reduced in the colon to a semi-solid consistency, the *feces*. When the muscular, terminal portion of the colon, the *rectum,* is filled, the feces are eliminated through the open anal sphincter. Feces are usually composed of 50 to 75 percent water in addition to cellulose, dead mucosal cells, and bacteria.

The Liver

This soft, multilobed organ, located just under the diaphragm (Fig. 8.1), is the largest gland in the body. The liver receives its blood supply directly from the small intestine. Functionally, it is the single most important

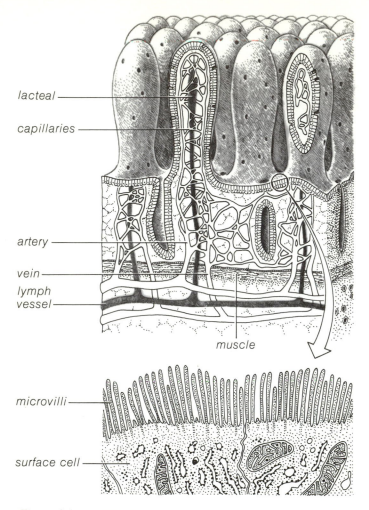

lacteal

capillaries

artery

vein

lymph vessel

muscle

microvilli

surface cell

Figure 8.2.   Villi lining the small intestine (top). Microvilli lining the surface of each villus (bottom). (From Kormondy et al.)

organ in the (intermediate) metabolism of all three major nutrients (i.e., fats, proteins, and carbohydrates). The liver converts glucose into the complex storage sugar, **glycogen,** which it also stores until it is needed. The liver forms the bile, which it releases into the gall bladder, where the bile is stored. In the complex metabolism of proteins, the liver converts amino acids into important antibodies and other protein components of blood. It is also an important center for the detoxification of drugs like morphine and of **steroid** hormones; it also converts uric acid into less acidic urea. (See Chapter 9.) Clearly, the normal functioning of the liver is highly essential to good health.

Aging of the Gastrointestinal System

The Mouth

Progressive loss of *teeth,* with time, due to caries and root and gum infections is a common occurrence. However, **periodontal** (gum) disease is the chief cause of tooth loss in later years. Either ill-fitting dentures or failure to replace lost teeth will result in poor mastication. This may likewise occur in cases of partial paralysis of the jaw from stroke or other causes. In such cases, the diet is often shifted to softer, usually semisolid foods. This, in turn, may result in an unbalanced diet and, consequently, malnutrition and vitamin and mineral deficiencies.

Older persons frequently suffer from a chronically dry mouth, a condition that may result from senile atrophy of the salivary glands and consequently in a reduction in the amount of saliva secreted, as well as increased alkalinity of their secretions. A dry mouth is also often associated with a shift to breathing through the mouth, a habit that may become chronic, especially in older persons with emphysema.

The Esophagus

Either neuromuscular impairment resulting from nervous disorders or, in extreme cases, cancer of the esophagus will produce difficulty in swallowing in older persons. In addition, the peristaltic movements of the esophagus slow down with age so that the time taken to move the food bolus from the pharynx to the stomach is prolonged. In more than 50 percent of older persons, the cardiac sphincter often fails to relax, further delaying the emptying of the esophageal contents into the stomach.

The Stomach

A common disorder in older persons is chronic inflammation of the lining of the stomach, due both to increasing atrophy of its mucous glands and its peptic glands with age. This condition, *atrophic* **gastritis,** is also characterized by a reduction in secretion of digestive juices in the stomach with age; in persons aged 60 or over, the reduction is 28 percent in men and is even higher in women. As Table 8.1 shows, *achlorhydria,* which is the failure to secrete hydrochloric acid essential to stomach digestion of proteins, increases steadily from ages 40 to 70 years in both men and women. The incidence of stomach cancer also increases with age. Although the frequency of gastric (stomach) ulcers increases in middle age, relatively few cases *develop* after age 60.

Table 8.1   Percentage Incidence of Achlorhydria in Different
                Age Groups

		Percentage Incidence of Achlorhydria	
Age	*Group*	*Males*	*Females*
40–49		9.9	13.0
50–59		18.2	18.0
60–69		23.1	27.6
70–79		20.0	19.4

Source: From Brocklehurst 1973, p. 327.

The Small Intestine

The weight of the small intestine decreases markedly after age 40 as a result of the continued atrophy of the mucous layer (the *mucosa*), the more internal layers (the *submucosa*), and the muscle tissue of its walls. Unfortunately, the accumulation of knowledge of changes in the small intestine and its functioning with age has been prevented by the rapid deterioration and difficulty in preservation of intestinal tissues after their excision. In general, however, there is a gradual decrease in the levels of the various intestinal enzymes, beginning as early as the third decade of life. The rate of intestinal absorption of monosaccharides, the simplest sugars, diminishes in later years. Similarly, the (active) transport of amino acids across the membrane wall of the small intestine into its capillary circulation is markedly reduced in old persons.

The Large Intestine

As one grows older, **constipation,** irregular and difficult passage of usually excessively dry feces, is more likely to occur. Constipation is a recurrent problem in about one-third of people 60 to 80 years of age. It is the result of the combined effects of decreased fluid intake and dietary bulk necessary to stimulate colonic motility. It may also be due to diminishing smooth muscle content and tone of the wall of the colon, plus decreased physical activity resulting from the sedentary life of older persons. Constipation may be exacerbated by hemorrhoids or the use of specific drugs for particular chronic diseases or both. This condition often results in an increasing dependence on laxatives, which, in turn, aggravates the problem of constipation even further.

Intestinal obstructions are more likely to occur in older individuals; the most extreme cases involve cancer of the small or large intestine.

Diverticulosis is a condition characterized by the presence of out-pocketings of the large intestine in an irregular fashion. Its incidence rises from 8 percent in men and women under 60 to 40 percent in persons over 70. However, it is responsible for only 3 percent of gastrointestinal disorders (see below). Diverticulosis produces considerable intestinal distress, including gas and local pain.

The Liver

The total weight of the liver diminishes gradually from 1600 grams at ages 21 to 30 to 1182 grams at ages 50 to 75 (about 20 percent). Yet 50 percent of the liver can be removed without appreciable reduction in effectiveness in its many complex functions. The liver does show, however, a decrease in its ability to metabolize certain drugs with age. This means that drug dosages for chronic ailments require adjustment according to age.

The Gall Bladder

This organ shows little change in function with age, although its walls do show atrophic shrinking, sclerosis, and thickening in older persons. The bile which it stores is more viscous and richer in cholesterol. The incidence of gallstones increases with age from 15 percent in men and 36 percent in women to 25 percent and 45 percent respectively, from 60 to 69 years of age.

Jaundice is a yellowing of the skin and eyes. It occurs with greater frequency in persons over 65. Eighty percent of cases of jaundice are due to the obstruction of bile flow, especially in malignancy (cancer); however, 16 percent of such cases are due to diseases of the liver itself.

Loss of Appetite

A common complaint in the ailing and frail elderly person, loss of appetite may be due to such serious conditions as incipient congestive heart failure, anemia, and cancer of the stomach. When present in otherwise healthy older persons, loss of appetite usually has a psychological or emotional basis. Such emotional problems can result, for example, from retirement, loss of employment, reduced income from these and other causes, or from an alteration in peer role or familial or social status. Other factors may include a fear of growing old, a fear of death, the loss of friends by death, or widowhood, especially in older men. In some people, however, boredom, insecurity, or unhappiness resulting from some of the above factors result in an *excessive* appetite.

Gastrointestinal Disorders

Disorders of the gastrointestinal system in the elderly are not necessarily different from those seen in young and mature persons. However, they are usually more serious and, of course, include an increasing incidence of cancer. Of the diseases of the alimentary canal in persons over 65, 56 percent represent *functional disorders* (i.e., there is no diagnosable organic basis), 10 percent represent malignancies, 8 percent gall bladder disease, 9 percent gastric and duodenal ulcers, and 3 percent diverticulosis. Functional disorders include hyperirritability or spasms of the lower intestinal tract, referred to as either irritable colon or spastic **colitis;** these occur especially in persons with emotional or psychological problems. Characteristic symptoms are heartburn, belching, nausea, and diarrhea. This condition may be accompanied by ulcers. The anxiety and depression seen in *senile dementia* or organic brain syndrome (see Chapter 5) are often accompanied by gastrointestinal disorders as well. Accordingly, management of the older patient with functional gastrointestinal disorders without any underlying, degenerative anatomical basis demands not only appropriate sedative or antispasmodic drugs and an appropriate adjustment in diet but also, most importantly, appropriate, supportive psychotherapy (Freeman 1965).

Summary

Structurally, the aging gastrointestinal tract is marked by senile atrophy of the mucous lining, the secretory glands, and the smooth muscle of its walls. Functionally, reduced motility and, therefore, a slowing of peristaltic movement, results in an increasing incidence of constipation with age. Diminished levels of digestive enzymes also occur, and a more viscous and more cholesterol-rich bile is produced. There is also an increased incidence of gallstones and of stomach and colonic cancer with advancing years. A variety of other gastrointestinal disorders increasingly occur, ranging from intestinal distress to diverticulosis to spastic colitis. Complicating the organic bases for such disorders is the common involvement of emotional and psychological problems of the older person that may be due to economic or social problems arising from retirement, widowhood, fear of dying, or the anxiety and depression arising from senile dementia. Accordingly, in addition to appropriate dietary adjustment and drug therapy, appropriate supportive psychotherapy may be required in the treatment of functional digestive disorders of the older patient.

References

Agate, J. 1963. The practice of geriatrics. Charles C. Thomas, Springfield, Ill., pp. 113–137.

Bhanthumnavin, K., and M. M. Schuster. 1977. Aging and gastrointestinal function. Pages 709–719 *in* C. E. Finch and L. Hayflick, eds., Handbook of the biology of aging. Van Nostrand Reinhold, New York.

Brocklehurst, J. C. 1973. The large bowel. Pages 346–363 *in* J. C. Brocklehurst, ed., Textbook of geriatric medicine and gerontology. Churchill Livingstone, Edinburgh and London.

Freeman, J. T., ed. 1965. Clinical features of the older patient. Charles C. Thomas Co., pp. 190–195.

Hyams, D. E. 1973. The liver and biliary system. Pages 364–383 *in* J. C. Brocklehurst, ed., Textbook of geriatric medicine and gerontology.

Leeming, J. T., S. P. G. Webster, and I. W. Bymock. 1973. Gastrointestinal system. Pages 321–345 *in* J. C. Brocklehurst, ed., Textbook of geriatric medicine and gerontology.

Sklar, M., J. B. Kirsner, and W. L. Palmer. 1965. G. I. disease. Pages 190–209 *in* J. T. Freeman, ed., Clinical features of the older patient. Charles C. Thomas, Springfield, Ill.

Tumen, H. J., and H. R. Clearfield. 1965. Jaundice. Pages 210–219 *in* J. T. Freeman, ed., Clinical features of the older patient.

Vanzant, F. R. 1932. The normal range of gastric acidity from youth to old age: An analysis of 3,746 records. Archives of Internal Medicine 49:345–359.

Zimmerman, K. 1965. Constipation. Pages 220–227 *in* J. T. Freeman, ed., Clinical features of the older patient.

Chapter Nine

The Urinary System

After reviewing the structure and function of the components of the urinary system, this chapter will focus on the effect of aging on the kidneys, the most important organs of the urinary system, and will then discuss urinary tract diseases and disorders in the elderly, including the causes of incontinence.

We have seen that, following digestion and absorption of nutrients and of vitamins and minerals, further processing then occurs in the liver. Blood from the liver is transported via the dorsal aorta by way of the renal arteries to the kidneys. The overall function of the kidneys is the maintenance of normal levels of water, salt, glucose, and the (mildly alkaline) pH of the blood. The urinary system as a whole serves to eliminate excesses of water and of inorganic and organic compounds, including the inert by-products of liver detoxification of noxious substances and the waste products of metabolism, such as *urea*.

Anatomy and Physiology

The urinary system includes the paired *kidneys,* the paired *ureters,* the tubes that transport the urine formed in the kidneys to the *bladder,* and the single terminal excretory tube, the **urethra** (Fig. 9.1).

The Kidneys

The kidneys are paired, bean-shaped organs located in the rear of the abdominal cavity on either side of vertebral column. Each kidney is covered by a thin collagenous capsule. Internally, the kidney is subdivided into an inner **medulla** and outer *cortex*. The nephron (kidney tubule) is the structural

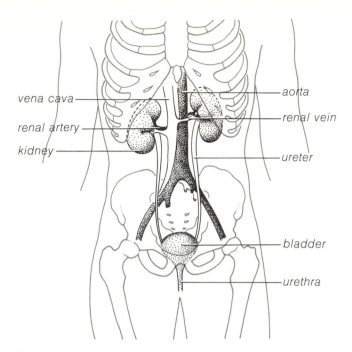

Figure 9.1.   The human excretory system and its relation to the major blood vessels. (From Kormondy et al.)

and functional unit of the kidney (Fig. 9.2). There are about one million nephrons in the young adult kidney. Located in the outer cortex of the kidney are the renal corpuscle and most of the convoluted tubule of each nephron. Each renal corpuscle consists of a *tuft* or mass of capillaries surrounded by a thin-walled capsule, known as Bowman's capsule. **Plasma** of the blood entering the kidney's capillaries is filtered from the glomerular tuft into the Bowman's capsule, which leads into the convoluted tubule. The distal tubules of the nephrons empty into the collecting tubules, which are located in the medulla of each kidney. These ducts in turn empty into the ureters and, finally, into the bladder.

It is along the various segments of kidney tubule that water and needed solutes (such as glucose, metallic ions, and various salts like bicarbonate and chloride) are reabsorbed into the capillaries and that unneeded substances are secreted into the forming urine. In this fashion, the original *glomerular plasma filtrate* is converted into urine to be excreted via the ureters and bladder. About 1200 to 1300 ml. of blood passes through each kidney per minute. About 50 percent of that volume is filtered from the glomeruli into the nephrons of each kidney as plasma. Of this 600 ml. of plasma, about 1 ml. per minute of urine is produced, or about 1.2 to 1.5 liters of urine per day in a young adult male.

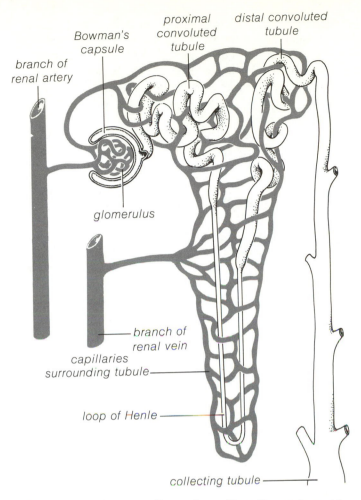

branch of
renal artery

Bowman's
capsule

proximal
convoluted
tubule

distal convoluted
tubule

glomerulus

branch of
renal vein

capillaries
surrounding tubule

loop of Henle

collecting tubule

Figure 9.2.   A mammalian nephron. (From Kormondy et al.)

The Ureters

Each of these 11-inch-long tubes consists of an inner mucous coat, a middle layer of inner circular and outer longitudinal muscles, and an outer fibrous coat. Peristaltic contractions of its wall transport the urine downward into the bladder.

The Bladder

This muscular sac located in the pubic region receives and stores the urine. It contracts into folds when empty; being highly distensible, it can hold up to 500 ml. of urine. Under normal conditions, the bladder fills slowly without opening of the sphincter into the *urethra*. This is due to the inhibitory control by the cerebral cortex of both the smooth muscle walls and the sphincter. In normal adults, when the volume of urine in the bladder reaches about 150 ml., appropriate nerve endings in the wall of the bladder begin to be stimulated, resulting in a conscious sensation of a need to empty the bladder. Depending on individual differences, voluntary urination (*micturition*) usually results when the bladder is half full. Micturition involves a voluntary relaxation of the bladder sphincter and contraction of the muscles of the wall of the bladder, which **voids** the bladder of its contents through the urethra.

Aging of the Kidneys

Anatomical Changes

Aging of the kidneys has been studied in considerable detail. From birth onward, they increase rapidly in size. Upon attaining a maximum weight of 270 grams by age 30, each kidney then shows a gradual decrease in weight to a minimum weight of two-thirds the maximum weight by age 90 (see Table 9.1). With age, the kidney becomes darker in color because of an increasing accumulation of pigment.

Within the *nephrons,* both the number of glomeruli as well as the total glomerular surface fall by over 50 percent from age 40 to 80. At the same time, the number of abnormal glomeruli rises from 5 percent to about 37 percent during this same period. Obsolescent glomeruli are replaced by the chemical **hyaline** as they are reabsorbed. Concomitantly, the muscular walls of the arteries that supply the kidney show the usual age changes, chiefly an increasing deposition of collagen and loss of muscle fibers.

Functional Changes

The **glomerular filtration** rate, that is, the rate at which plasma is filtered out of the blood passing through the kidneys, i.e., from the glomeruli

Table 9.1   Age Changes in Kidney Weight (Both Kidneys)

Age	Kidney Weight
At birth	50 gm.
30–40 yrs.	270 gm.
60 yrs.	250 gm.
70 yrs.	230 gm.
80 yrs.	190 gm.

Source: Data from Goldman 1977 and Sourander 1973.

into Bowman's capsule, is the most significant measure of renal function. It falls steadily from 140 ml. per minute per 1.73 square meters of body surface at age 21 to 97 ml. at age 80. Other more specific measurements are **renal plasma flow** and *proximal tubular function.* Whereas the glomerular filtration rate declines by about 0.7 percent per year, the renal plasma flow falls by 0.9 percent per year, and the proximal tubular function by 0.65 to 0.68 percent per year. As tubular function declines, the urine accordingly becomes less concentrated as the individual ages, the specific gravity or density decreasing from 1.030 at age 40 to 1.023 at age 90.

Urinary Tract Diseases and Disorders

Infectious Diseases. Kidney diseases account for a significant number of hospital visits by the elderly. **Pyelonephritis,** an infection of the kidney, is the most common renal complication of the aged male. Other fairly common complaints are infections of the urethra, bladder, and, in more severe cases, of the kidney tubules themselves. In fact, second only to pulmonary infections, renal infection is one of the most common causes of fever in older persons, especially men. Such infections are often accompanied by *oliguria,* a reduction in urine output to less than 300 ml. daily.

Incontinence. The ability of the bladder to store urine diminishes at advanced ages without any apparent anatomical basis. Accordingly, the frequency of voiding (*micturition*) increases. The volume of urine remaining in the bladder after voiding also increases with age. For example, as we have seen earlier, in youth the need to void occurs when the bladder is about half full. In the older person, this sensation occurs when the bladder is nearly full. This results in frequent and, commonly, nocturnal micturition in 70 percent of men and 61 percent of women over 65. At the same time, the inability to maintain control of the bladder sphincter to the urethra (seen in 28 percent of men and 32 percent of women over 65) results in incontinence. This combination of factors not uncommonly results in bedwetting in advanced old age. It is especially common in persons suffering from senile dementia or organic brain syndrome or as part of the post-injury **sequelae** of stroke (cerebrovascular accident).

Another less common symptom of urinary system dysfunction in older persons is more or less *completely* uncontrolled or involuntary voiding, occurring in 3 percent of older women and 13 percent of men over 65. In males, this symptom is often associated with hypertrophy of the prostate gland from benign or malignant causes.

Summary

Renal function changes with age include a gradual diminution in glomerular filtration rate, renal plasma flow, renal tubular function, and urine concentration. However, the reduction in these functions does not constitute a major problem in the elderly. Kidney disease, especially *lower* and, less frequently, *upper* urinary tract and bladder infections are a common complaint among the elderly, especially older men.

Bladder function commonly undergoes age-related changes. These changes include an increase in frequency of urination and in the residual volume of urine in the bladder following each voiding. Incontinence and bedwetting likewise become increasingly greater problems with age, particularly in persons with lesions of the cerebral cortex and organic brain syndrome.

References

Brocklehurst, J. C. 1973. The bladder. Pages 298–320 *in* J. C. Brocklehurst, ed., Textbook of geriatric medicine and gerontology. Churchill Livingstone, Edinburgh and London.

Davies, D. F., and N. W. Shock. 1950. Age changes in the glomerular filtration rate, effective renal plasma flow, and tubular excretory capacity in adult males. Journal of Clinical Investigation 29:496–506.

Goldman, R. 1977. Aging of the excretory system: Kidney and bladder. Pages 409–431 *in* C. E. Finch and L. Hayflick, eds., Handbook of the biology of aging. Van Nostrand Reinhold, New York.

Lindeman, R. D. 1975. Age changes in renal function. Pages 19–38 *in* R. Goldman, M. Rockstein, and M. Sussman, eds., The physiology and pathology of human aging. Academic Press, New York.

Miller, J. H., R. K. McDonald, and N. W. Shock. 1952. Age changes in the maximal rate of renal tubular reabsorption of glucose. Journal of Gerontology 7:196–200.

Rowe, J. W., R. Andres, J. D. Tobin, A. H. Norris, and N. W. Shock. 1976. The effect of age on creatinine clearance in man: A cross-sectional and longitudinal study. Journal of Gerontology 31:155–163.

Sourander, L. B. 1973. The aging kidney. Pages 280–297 *in* J. C. Brocklehurst, ed., Textbook of geriatric medicine and gerontology. Churchill Livingstone, Edinburgh and London.

Chapter Ten

Nutrition

Of all the environmental factors affecting the quality of life, nutrition may well be the most important. However, the precise role of diet in the human aging process is still "little known" (Watkin 1976) because of the complex interaction of such factors as economic status, bereavement, and physical state in determining the progress of the aging process. Moreover, in any segment of the population, but especially in the elderly, individual nutritional needs vary widely according to one's body structure, metabolism, level of physical activity and, most importantly, state of health.

This chapter will (1) discuss the role of malnutrition in the aging process, (2) detail the factors governing the quality of dietary intake, (3) review the recommended dietary intake, and (4) critically discuss the fads and facts concerning the use of specific foods in attempts to retard the aging process.

Unfortunately, the term malnutrition often evokes an image of starving people in underdeveloped nations. In actual fact, malnutrition is improper nutrition from any cause, ranging from starvation to a poor diet to overnourishment. Indeed, overnourishment may be a more significant contributory factor to early morbidity (disease) than is undernourishment, especially in western nations. At the same time, few physicians stress the importance of diet in the prevention of specific diseases having nutritional involvements, such as heart disease and atherosclerosis.

On a global scale, there is no question that undernourishment and starvation contribute to a reduction of life span. For example, in countries like India, average longevities are 10 to 20 years less than those of most western countries, and of Japan, Russia, and Israel. The shorter average life span in countries like India is related to a lowered resistance to life-shortening diseases like tuberculosis.

Malnutrition in the Elderly

In the United States, on the other hand, the incidence of nutritionally related diseases (due chiefly to inadequate intake of essential nutrients) is especially prominent in the elderly. The reduced income of the retirement population is partially responsible for this inadequate diet. However, even when financial assistance (such as food stamps) is available from local or federal sources, older persons commonly experience malnutrition for other reasons. Poor health, for example, may simply limit the physical ability of the older person to go marketing. Chronic illness or the effects of drugs employed in its treatment may also reduce one's desire for food. Likewise, loss of teeth or, where corrected, poorly fitting dentures may affect one's desire for food or, at best, limit the kind of food normally eaten. The resulting preponderance of soft foods in the diet in place of meats and fresh fruits and vegetables, means not only a poorly balanced diet but also, not uncommonly, constipation (see Chapter 8).

Older persons often show a disinterest in food for emotional reasons. Changes both in income and one's peer role which come with retirement are particularly damaging to the morale of the newly retired person. Traditionally, this has been especially true of the retired man, who has enjoyed the status resulting from his role as the primary wage earner in the family and as a peer in business, in his profession, in government service, or other work environment. These factors are equally applicable to the increasing number of women who assume wage-earning and career roles. Also, the depression following the loss of a spouse, particularly in the older man who is unaccustomed to preparing meals, frequently results in the rejection of food. Similarly, the isolation from friends and family resulting from emigration to another region often leads to feelings of loneliness and depression and, in turn, a loss of desire for food, irregular meals, and inadequate nutrition.

Finally, for various reasons, many people who live alone find it difficult to prepare meals for only one person. Thus, the elderly consumer may make use of easily consumable foods that require little or no preparation, such as cakes, breads, crackers, and T.V. dinners. These foods may provide a quick, easy, and relatively inexpensive way to satisfy hunger, but, even when supplemented by vitamins and minerals, essential nutrients such as high-quality protein may be lacking in such a diet. Moreover, foods prepared in mass kitchens for delivery to older people at home or in institutions may have lost some of their nutritional value, especially during their preparation.

Factors in Nutrition

For human beings and all other animals, the daily intake of food must include a proper balance of the three essential nutrients: carbohydrates, fats, and proteins. Moreover, the total amount of such a balanced diet should include enough **calories** to meet the metabolic needs of the individual without producing obesity. Although norms of dietary needs have been established, it is obvious that the individual's sex, weight, height, physical activity, genetic make-up, social environment, and economic status affect a person's nutritional requirements. Differences in nutritional requirements resulting from these individual variables occur in all age groups but to a greater degree among the elderly (Table 10.1). That is, the caloric requirements of this segment of the population vary in relation to three basic factors: **basal metabolic rate,** physical activity, and efficiency of movement.

Basal metabolic rate.   This is a measure of the amount of energy required by the body at rest. This value is reduced by 5 percent every 10 years between the ages of 35 and 55, by 8 percent per decade between 55 and 75, and by 10 percent per decade thereafter.

Physical activity.   Variations in daily physical activity mean differences in the daily expenditure of energy and, therefore, caloric requirements even among people in the same age group. For example, older men (aged 55 to 72 years) working in light engineering expend about 2900 calories per day whereas those in heavy engineering require 3300 calories per day. Any alteration in the intensity of physical activity, such as that which occurs at retirement from a job, in a reduction in household chores, when children leave home, or with a reduction in the scope and intensity of leisure time activities due to neurological deficits of old age, may result in a corresponding decrease in nutritional requirements, particularly caloric intake.

Efficiency of movement.   This factor likewise is important in determining caloric requirements since about one-third of the daily caloric intake is expended on muscular activity. The efficiency with which food energy is used to drive muscle movements is reduced in the elderly. That is, it usually takes more energy for an older person than a younger one to do comparable work. One study (Table 10.1) has shown that certain exercises require the

Table 10.1   Mean Energy Expenditure (cal./min) of Young and Elderly Subjects during Standard Exercise Regimens

Exercise	Young (20–30 years)	Elderly (55–67 years)	Percentage Difference
Light (arm ergometer)	4.12	4.36	+ 5.8%
Moderate (treadmill)	5.72	6.68	+16.8%
Heavy (treadmill)	7.04	8.50	+20.7%

Source: Adapted from Durnin and Mikulcic 1956.

expenditure of significantly higher levels of energy in the elderly. Under conditions of light exercise, the differences between the young men (aged 20 to 30) and older men (55 to 67) were not significant. However, for moderate to heavy exercise involving greater total body muscle activity, the older men expended significantly greater energy.

Nutritional Requirements of the Elderly

Calories

The daily caloric requirements of older individuals are much less than those of young persons. For men, caloric requirements decrease only slightly in their final working years, with an abrupt drop to 2300 calories per day after retirement. Energy requirements for women are more difficult to determine, because of greater variation in the life styles of women. After age 60, most women require between 1500 and 2000 calories a day (see Table 10.2). Accordingly, as a general guideline, some clinicians recommend a voluntary reduction in caloric intake of 3 percent per decade between the ages of 25 and 45 and of 7.5 percent per decade from 45 to 65. Thereafter, a reduction of 10 percent per decade is suggested.

Protein

The amount of protein required daily to maintain muscle mass does not diminish appreciably with advancing age. The accepted figure for all adults varies slightly from study to study (Table 10.3). There is limited evidence that indicates that the requirement for nitrogen, one of the essential elements of proteins, may increase in men over age 50. In times of illness or stress, however, the requirement for protein may increase in all persons. Since the elderly are more prone to these conditions, their protein requirements may be slightly higher than those of young and middle-aged persons.

Table 10.2   Caloric Requirements (cal./day) for Various Activities of People 60 Years of Age

Activity	Men	Women
Resting (basal)	1500	1250
Sedentary work	2000	1750
Light work	2500	2000

Source: Adapted from various sources. (See Reference List)

Table 10.3   Protein Requirements of the Elderly

Study	*Age*	*Sex*	*Estimated Requirements (gm./kg./day)*
A	41–86	Male	Less than 1.0
B	69–76	Male	0.7
C	61–79	Male	0.5
D	50–75	Female	0.9

Source: Adapted from Barrows and Roeder 1977.

Inadequate protein intake is a particularly common occurrence among the elderly, due to poor dentition and to the economic and other factors discussed above. One study indicated that 4 percent of the elderly patients admitted to a hospital with **edema** (swelling due to increased fluid in the tissues) were suffering from inadequate protein intake (Durnin and Mikulcic 1956).

Carbohydrates

Carbohydrates are the source of quick energy since the calories they contain may be rapidly used by the body. Adequate carbohydrate content in the diet spares the use of body fat stores and structural proteins for energy. On the other hand, when a person fasts, the carbohydrate, glycogen, usually stored in amounts of several hundred grams in the liver and in muscle tissue, is immediately metabolized. When these sources are exhausted, further fasting causes stored fat to be metabolized. Under conditions of severe longterm caloric restriction, after fat reserves are depleted, structural proteins (e.g., muscle) are used. The severely undernourished individual has little, if any, stored carbohydrate or fat and survives chiefly by metabolizing structural proteins. Unfortunately, many persons, especially the elderly, eat diets high in carbohydrates but without adequate levels of protein and essential fats.

Fats

The human body can synthesize many *unsaturated fats* (fats that tend to be less solid) in the liver. However, certain fatty acids that are the building blocks of long fat molecules are not synthesized in humans and must be obtained from the diet.

Unsaturated fatty acids are essential to the diet since they are used in the body to manufacture a fatty compound called *cholesterol* (a **precursor** of many hormones). With advancing age, there is a general elevation in the cholesterol levels in the blood of people on normal diets. Some clinicians believe that high blood cholesterol levels are indirectly related to the development of atherosclerosis (Chapter 6). However, it is diets rich in **saturated fats** which may cause the body to produce compounds called *cholesterol esters*. These compounds are deposited in the walls of blood vessels, causing atherosclerosis. Serum cholesterol levels may rise after eating a meal rich in fats. It is interesting to note that such arterial disease does not begin in old age since it is, in part, the result of the dietary habits of a lifetime. Many physicians believe that the proper balance of saturated to unsaturated fats in youth and middle age may retard the progress of atherosclerosis in later life. Few people, however, worry about this condition before the signs of the disease appear. Yet, a 60-year-old person (with a life expectancy of 21 additional years) might be able to slow the progress of the disease with dietary adjustments even at this late stage of life. Since the elderly tend to resist any kind of change in long-established habits, many may be unwilling to alter their diets even for health reasons. Such a person may experience a heart attack or related heart problems before becoming sufficiently concerned to alter his or her diet.

Vitamins

Vitamins are organic molecules (other than carbohydrates, proteins, or fats) that are not manufactured in the body but are required in minute quantities for normal bodily metabolism. Vitamins play important roles in a variety of vital processes such as the metabolism of fats, proteins, and carbohydrates, resistance to infection, the healing of wounds, vision, and blood clotting, to name a few. Vitamin requirements depend on a person's size, stage of growth, activity, and health. Exercise or illness may actually increase the body's vitamin requirements.

Most nutritionists correctly suggest that the nutritional requirements of the elderly are no different from those of younger individuals with the minor exceptions noted earlier, namely their lower daily requirements of caloric intake (Table 10.4). Moreover, inasmuch as vitamin requirements are related to caloric intake, they should, likewise, be lower than that of young people. The decrease in the number of actively metabolizing cells with advancing age may also reduce the body's vitamin requirements at the cellular level. In fact, few studies have conclusively resolved the question of specific vitamin requirements for older persons. Accordingly, there is no real evidence for the general recommendation of vitamin supplements for *all* older people nor for the common practice among the elderly of routinely taking multivitamin tablets. In fact, some fat-soluble vitamins (e.g., vitamin A) when taken in high doses may cause detrimental changes in bone and blood vessels.

The incidence of vitamin deficiencies among the older American population is lower than for similar populations in other countries. This is

Table 10.4   Recommended Dietary Allowances (RDA) for Persons over 50 Years of Age

	Women	*Men*
Calories	1800.0	2400.0
Protein (gm.)	46.0	56.0
Vitamin A (International Units, IU)	4000.0	5000.0
Vitamin E (IU)	12.0	15.0
Vitamin C (IU)	45.0	45.0
Niacin (mg.)	12.0	16.0
Riboflavin (mg.)	1.1	1.5
Thiamine (mg.)	1.0	1.2
Calcium (mg.)	800.0	800.0
Iron (mg.)	10.0	10.0

Source: National Research Council 1974.

due, in part, to the comparatively high level of nutrition of Americans in general.

Vitamin deficiencies in the elderly usually go hand in hand with the generally inadequate nutrition that may result from a number of causes already discussed. For example, the older person may eat less meat, a major source of the B-complex vitamins, because of its high cost or because of an inability to chew it. Special diets necessary for persons with certain chronic diseases (such as ulcers) often require vitamin supplementation. Indeed, Watkin, one of the foremost authorities in the field of nutrition, has stated that "disease rather than diet" must be the primary consideration in nutrition for the aging.[1] Even in government-sponsored nutritional programs for the elderly ostensibly insuring adequate vitamin content in the diet, some persons exhibited vitamin B-complex or C deficiencies.

Finally, chronic alcoholism, an ever-increasing problem especially among the aged, is a source of severe vitamin deficiencies, as alcohol is substituted for a well-balanced nutritious diet.

Vitamin A maintains the *epithelial* cells of the skin; it is particularly important in eye physiology and in skeletal development. It may be stored by the body for many months, so care must be taken to prevent overdose when vitamin supplements are taken. Failure of bile secretion, laxative use, antibiotics and some drugs all decrease the absorption of vitamin A.

Carrots, spinach, brussels sprouts, broccoli, and tomatoes are rich sources of vitamin A. Early experimental studies suggested that elevated levels of vitamin A intake are beneficial to older humans. Thus, subjects receiving fewer than 5000 IU (international units) had a 13.9 percent mortal-

[1]Watkin, D. M., 1977; personal communication.

ity, those receiving 5000–7999 IU a 6.9 percent mortality, and those receiving 8000+ IU had a 4.3 percent mortality. However, longterm overdosage may lead to liver damage.

Vitamin B1 (thiamine) is involved in carbohydrate metabolism. Thus, its requirements are directly correlated with the amount of carbohydrate intake. Thiamine deficiency causes loss of appetite, exhaustion, and changes in mental states (i.e., increased anxiety). Extreme deficiency causes *beri beri,* a disease uncommon in the United States. Thiamine is necessary for the synthesis of certain *coenzymes.* The body does not store this vitamin in any appreciable amount. Whole grain cereals, enriched bread, and pork and beef are good sources of thiamine. Elderly persons existing on high-carbohydrate, low-protein diets may be deficient in thiamine, and dietary supplementation could be necessary. Thiamine may be destroyed by heat and therefore lost during cooking.

Vitamin B6 (**pyridoxine**) is involved in antibody formation and protein metabolism. Extreme deficiencies result in loss of appetite and weight, general weakness, skin problems, nausea, vomiting, and dizziness. Vitamin B6 is widely distributed in whole grain cereals, pork, liver, and vegetables. Deficiencies are uncommon in humans, except in the case of very poor diets. Toxicity has been reported for persons receiving more than 300 mg. per day.

Niacin (nicotinic acid and niacinamide) is known to prevent the disease *pellagra.* Its deficiency is marked by loss of appetite, digestive disturbances, irritability, anxiety, and depression. Niacin is commonly found in lean meat, cereal bran, wheat germ, whole grains, legumes (beans and peas), and yeast. Thus, pellagra is associated with lack of whole grains in the diet.

Riboflavin is essential for oxidation in the tissues and is important in protein synthesis and tissue metabolism. Its deficiency produces local tissue changes such as lesions of the mouth, lips, and eyes. It is a heat-stable vitamin, found in milk, especially, and in green vegetables, liver, fish, and eggs.

Vitamin B12 (**cyanocobalamin**) is essential for normal functioning of the central nervous system, the gastrointestinal tract, and the bone marrow in the production of red blood cells. Its deficiency results in pernicious anemia, lesions of the tongue (*glossitis*) and mouth, and lesions of the spinal cord. It is found in foods of animal origin, especially liver and kidney. Negligible quantities of vitamin B12 are found in vegetables. In fact, persons living exclusively on vegetarian diets may have signs of glossitis and lesions of the spinal cord, but rarely anemia. Since this vitamin is found in more expensive foods such as meats and fish that the elderly may omit from their diet, this group may develop vitamin B12 deficiency.

Folic acid (folacin) is involved in the production of the red and white cells of the blood and enhances the absorption of iron. Its deficiency results in diarrhea, anemia, and glossitis. It is present in dark green leafy vegetables, especially spinach, and in liver. It may be partially destroyed if stored for extended periods of time, and by cooking. Folic acid deficiency occurs most commonly among alcoholics with cirrhosis of the liver, and among the poor and persons over 65 years of age.

Vitamin C (**ascorbic acid**) has many functions in the body, all involving oxidation reactions. It participates in the regulation of the respiratory cycle in the cells and is involved in the maintenance of mechanical strength of blood vessels. Its deficiency leads to *scurvy,* a disease characterized by bleeding of the gums and sometimes hemorrhaging of other tissues. Adult males and pregnant or lactating females require about 60 mg. of vitamin C per day. Adult women need about 55 mg. daily. Except where massive daily doses are taken, vitamin C overdose is rare, since excess vitamin C is excreted in the urine when saturation levels are reached.

Ascorbic acid is present in foods such as citrus fruits, juices, tomatoes, and other vegetables. Eggs, meats, and fish are poor sources. Vitamin C is often added to processed beverages. Food processing often destroys this water-soluble vitamin, and, unless fresh vegetables and fruits are eaten or vitamin supplements taken, vitamin C deficiencies are possible. Since older people may find it difficult to market regularly, they often use preserved foods instead of more perishable fresh fruits and vegetables, so that a supplement of vitamin C may be necessary.

Vitamin D is involved in maintaining the balance of the chemical elements in bone tissue—calcium and phosphate. Its deficiency in children may cause rickets and in adults the corresponding condition, **osteomalacia.** There is evidence that vitamin D may be involved in calcium metabolism in the disease **osteoporosis** (described in Chapter 11). Since the body stores vitamin D, care must be taken to prevent overdose of this vitamin, or calcium overloading of the blood and other tissues can result.

Vitamin E (**alpha-tocopherol**), not an essential nutrient in man, is in fact a term applied to a group of compounds called "tocopherols." Although its function is not clearly defined, it is said to serve as an anti-oxidant (see Chapter 4). Its deficiency produces sterility in rats. The requirements for vitamin E in the diet may, accordingly, depend on the amount of polyunsaturated fat in the diet. Vitamin E is found in meats, milk, eggs, fish, wheat germ, and leafy vegetables. The general range of recommended adult daily needs for this vitamin is 10–30 mg. per day.

Vitamin K is involved in regulating the blood level of *prothrombin,* a compound important in the clotting of blood. It occurs in many foods, and so dietary deficiency of vitamin K in humans is quite rare.

For further information on the role of vitamins in general, see Latham et al. 1972, Mickelson 1976, and Todhunter 1971.

Minerals

Calcium plays an important role in bone and muscle physiology. Calcium deficiency has been suggested as a factor in senile **osteoporosis** (loss in bone mass due to demineralization). However, Garn has stated that calcium supplementation in the diet fails to reverse the symptoms of this serious bone disease (in Goldman, Rockstein, and Sussman 1975). The recommended dietary allowance for calcium in persons 50 years of age and over is 800 mg. per day.

Iron is particularly important in the diet as the central atom in the hemoglobin molecule of red blood cells that transport oxygen in the blood to all tissues of the body. The diet should provide about 10 mg. of iron each day. Inadequate intake of this mineral will lead to iron deficiency anemia, colloquially called "tired blood." Pathological conditions in some elderly people prevent the absorption of iron, as when, for example, the stomach produces decreased levels of acid (a condition called *achlorhydria*). In such cases, the daily requirements for iron may be considerably higher. Similarly, when iron is lost by hemorrhage, levels of iron intake may have to be increased through dietary supplements of meats, liver, beets, and other iron-rich foods.

Trace elements are minerals which are required in minute amounts. They are needed chiefly in catalytic (enzyme) reactions in all tissues throughout the body. Although some of the trace elements may be unfamiliar to the reader, the most common—iodine, cobalt, copper, fluorine, zinc, and manganese—are all necessary in small amounts in human nutrition. One of the less common trace elements, selenium, is essential for vitamin E and peroxidase (an enzyme) metabolism in the laboratory rat, several domestic animals, and possibly humans. Among a number of other trace elements tested to determine their influence on longevity in rats and mice, minute quantities of chromium, titanium, and niobium were found to promote growth. Germanium, on the other hand, produced a significantly shorter life span in mice. Fluorine, a trace element now added to the water supplies of many communities to prevent tooth decay, is effective in preventing calcium loss from bone. As such, it may be effective in preventing bone loss (osteoporosis) which occurs gradually with age.

"Hard water," that is, water high in dissolved minerals, may contain as many as 11 chemical constituents and 7 trace elements, but their concentration and incidence are subject to regional variation. A reduction in the mortality rate from cardiovascular disease, hypertensive heart disease, cerebral vascular lesions, and arteriosclerotic heart disease has been noted in regions supplied by hard water. Some people have even proposed that a "water factor" exists that is beneficial to health. However, the observed reduction in mortality from these diseases is probably due to a combination of trace elements rather than any single, specific factor in the water.

Obesity

The overabundance of foods rich in carbohydrates and fat combined with a lack of will power to restrict their intake and a lack of physical exercise all contribute to the incidence of obesity among the general population. From childhood, many people are taught that they must eat three well-balanced meals every day. However, as discussed earlier, nutritional requirements decrease as we get older. All of these factors contribute to the incidence of obesity among the elderly. Basic causes for extreme obesity include overeating for psychological reasons, childhood overnutrition, and hypothalamic abnormalities.

It is well known that during stressful situations people may eat excessively as a compensation or release from tension. Extreme obesity, in other than the unusual cases of endocrine dysfunction, is commonly the result of such *psychogenic overeating*. In such cases, psychiatric therapy can help control the weight problem.

A little known fact is that the number of fat cells in the body of an adult has been fully determined during childhood when such cells form. Thus, overnutrition particularly during infancy and, to a lesser degree, in later childhood results in a large number of fat cells in the body. In this case, obesity in later life is due to the superabundance of these early-established cells for later fat deposition when the fat and carbohydrate content of the diet is excessive.

Infrequently, abnormal functioning of the **hypothalamus,** a small structure at the base of the brain, may be the cause of excessive eating and extreme obesity. In most cases of extreme obesity, however, postmortem autopsy rarely reveals an abnormality of this organ (see Chapter 12).

Extreme obesity often plays a secondary or contributory role in numerous health problems associated with different organ systems of the body. These include difficulties in respiration (**dyspnea,** bronchitis), in metabolism (**diabetes mellitus,** gallstones, gout), and in circulation (high blood pressure, atherosclerosis, heart disease). The obese person with poor balance may also be more prone to accidents from which the severity of injury and recovery time may be greater than in the non-obese.

The importance of health problems due to being overweight is reflected in insurance statistics that emphasize a correlation between obesity and reduced life expectancy. For example, a 25-pound increase in weight above the standard for height and body build is said to reduce the life expectancy of a 45-year-old man by as much as 25 percent. The severity of this problem may be realized when you consider that the chances of dying from lung cancer after smoking 25 cigarettes per day for many years are lower than the morbidity rate for persons only 14 pounds overweight. In fact, if all the health problems associated with obesity and its related diseases were eliminated, a 4-year increase in mean longevity could be expected.

Dietary Manipulation of Disease States

The influence of diet specifically on the diseases of the elderly has been demonstrated in a 3-year Spanish study (Vallejo 1957). Healthy residents of an old people's residence facility were separated into two groups of 60 men and 60 women each. The experimental group received a diet containing 2300 calories daily, with 50 grams of protein and 40 grams of fat on *odd* days of the month, and 1 liter of cow's milk and 500 grams of fresh fruit on *even* days. The control group received the above diet *every* day. The group on the restricted diet (experimental) was healthier; they spent a total of 123 days in the infirmary and had 6 deaths during a 3-year period. The control group on the unrestricted diet spent 219 days in the infirmary and had 13 deaths during the same period.

Summary

Older persons are a group in our population who need and could benefit from nutritional counseling. Factors acting on the elderly population that are barriers to adequate nutrition include the following:

1. Limited income may restrict the purchase of adequate amounts of the proper foods. It may also fail to provide for adequate cooking and refrigeration facilities.
2. Appetite is usually reduced due to many different factors such as medications or psychological problems like loneliness, anxiety, or depression. Reduced physical activity, increased fatigue and weakness, or solitary living arrangements may also reduce the individual's desire to eat.
3. Poor teeth or inadequate dentures may limit the variety of foods that can be easily chewed.

References

Barrows, C. H., and L. M. Roeder. 1977. Nutrition. Pages 561–581 *in* C. E. Finch and L. Hayflick, eds., The handbook of the biology of aging. Van Nostrand Reinhold, New York.

Durnin, J.V.G., and C. V. Mikulcic. 1956. The influence of graded exercises on oxygen consumption, pulmonary ventilation and heart rate in young and elderly men. Quarterly Journal of Experimental Physiology 41:442–452.

Freeman, J. T. 1965. Nutrition. Pages 377–389 *in* J. T. Freeman, ed., Clinical features of the older patient. Charles C. Thomas, Springfield, Ill.

Garn, S. M. 1975. Bone loss and aging. Pages 39–57 *in* R. Goldman, M. Rockstein, and M. L. Sussman, eds., The physiology and pathology of human aging. Academic Press, New York.

Latham, M. C., R. B. McGandy, M. B. McCann, and F. J. Stare. 1972. Scope manual on nutrition. The Upjohn Co., Kalamazoo. 94 pp.

Mickelson, O. 1976. The possible role of vitamins in the aging process. Pages 123–142 *in* M. Rockstein and M. L. Sussman, eds., Nutrition, longevity and aging. Academic Press, New York.

National Research Council. 1974. Recommended dietary allowances, 8th rev. ed. National Academy of Science, Washington, D.C.

Rockstein, M., and M. L. Sussman, eds. 1976. Nutrition, longevity and aging. Academic Press, New York. 283 pp.

Todhunter, E. N. 1971. Nutrition: Background and issues. Pages 1–35 *in* Report of the Technical Committee on Nutrition, D. M. Watkin, ed. White House Conference on Aging, Washington, D.C.

Vallejo, E. A. 1957. La dieta de hombre a dias alternos en la alimentacion de los viejos. Prensa Medica Argentina 44:119.

Watkin, D. M. 1976. Biochemical impact of nutrition on the aging process. Pages 47–66 *in* M. Rockstein and M. L. Sussman, eds., Nutrition, longevity, and aging. Academic Press, New York.

Chapter Eleven

The Skin, Bone, and Muscle

The most easily observable changes that occur in aging are those of the skin, bone, and muscle. An older person develops wrinkled skin, graying or sparse hair, and sagging flesh, the effects of which are probably more damaging to psychological than to physical well-being. Also characteristic of an aged person are a stooped posture, slow, unsteady movements, and general weakening of muscle strength. All of these limit the physical activities and capabilities of the older person. In this chapter, we will examine the structural and functional changes in the skin, bone, and muscle underlying all these observable changes and will touch on the more important disorders of each of these organs that may occur among the elderly.

The Skin

Of all the organ systems of the body, the skin is most readily accessible for the study of age changes. Yet it is difficult to differentiate between normal aging of the skin, and the cumulative effects of such elements of the environment as wind, sun, and abrasion. Degenerative age changes in the skin, however, play little if any role in determining the aging and survival of the total body. Characteristically, aging skin becomes increasingly wrinkled, dry, and sagging. The hair becomes sparser and turns gray. The fingernails become duller, more opaque, and yellowish in appearance.

The Epidermis

The outer layers of the skin, the **epidermis,** show progressive atrophic changes with age. This is due in part to its lifelong exposure to environmental insults and is also related to the fact that the cells of the epidermal layers exhibit a decreased rate of cell division with advancing age. Thus, there is a diminished ability to replace damaged or dead cells. Unlike its importance to animals living in the wild, the resulting slower healing of wounds in older persons has relatively little significance.

Pigment cells of the epidermis (**melanocytes**) decrease by about 80 percent in number from age 27 to 65 (about 20 percent per decade). Those that remain tend to be larger. The sizeable, pronounced **pigment plaques** which appear in the skin of some persons in later years are thought to be produced by the aggregation of melanocytes.

The Dermis

The deeper layers of the skin, the **dermis,** show characteristic and essentially irreversible atrophic changes. Fine elastic fibers in the fetus become increasingly coarse in the young and older adult. In old persons, the elastin becomes increasingly cross-linked and calcified. Collagen content changes, and fat and water content diminish with age. These changes produce wrinkles and cause the skin to sag.

Sweat Glands.   The sweat glands and associated blood vessels show age-related atrophy. The sweat glands diminish in number and lipofuscin pigment granules accumulate slowly but progressively. Decreased output of sweat is a distinctive characteristic of older men and women.

The Hair.   Reduction in the pigment content of the hair usually begins in the late thirties or early forties. Graying begins in the temple regions, extending slowly to the vertex (top of the head). The onset, rate, and extent of graying however, may vary widely among individuals.

Hair loss is age-related in persons of either sex. The density of hair follicles falls from 615 per square centimeter at 25 years to 485 by age 50. Baldness, on the other hand, which is both genetically predetermined and age-related, usually begins earlier in life. Being sex-limited, it is rare in women. Nevertheless, baldness does progress with advancing age, following a common pattern of loss. It begins with the vertex and frontal-lateral regions and proceeds with a slow recession of the anterior hair line.

The Nails.   The rate of growth of the thumbnail declines from 0.83 mm. per week in the third decade to 0.52 mm. per week in the ninth decade, a 38 percent decrease. The growth of men's nails is faster than women's until the sixth decade, but then levels off during the seventh and into the eighth decade. Thereafter, nail growth in men falls below that of women. Senile nails are ridged, dull, opaque, and yellowish to greenish-gray, and are more prone to splitting into layers.

Skin Diseases in the Elderly

Diseases of the skin in older men and women include a variety of relatively common *dermatoses* (skin disorders). They may, however, be increasingly severe with age. Patchy eczema and psoriasis are the most common skin problems. Skin reactions to drugs like penicillin or barbiturates or to combinations of certain drugs are more likely to occur in older persons because of the greater occurrence of chronic drug therapy.

Psychological Aspects

The increasing lines and wrinkles in the skin and sagging flesh often have a pronounced effect on one's morale and feelings of self-worth. As the older population has grown in numbers, surgical "rejuvenation" (facial and body "plastic surgery") has become increasingly popular in middle age and beyond, especially among women. Without doubt, this has helped to revive or maintain a successful emotional and sexual relationship between some aging husbands and wives (see Chapter 14).

Bone

Age Changes

Calcium and phosphate mineralization of bone takes place during the maturation process and is generally completed by sexual maturity. Some postmaturational bone growth does take place in the form of widening of the limb bones well into middle age and later. Demineralization and loss of supporting bone matrix is characteristic of aging bone. This age-related, progressive bone loss results in a lighter total bone mass in older persons. As the bone becomes increasingly porous, it becomes more brittle. In extreme, clinically evident cases, such bone degeneration is called *osteoporosis*. Fractures are more common in older persons as a result. Some degree of collapse of the vertebral (spinal) bones results in a gradual diminution of stature in aging humans.

Bone loss with age is much greater in women than in men. Over a period of 30 years (55 to 85), women showed a 25 percent loss versus a 12 percent bone loss for men (Garn 1975). Moreover, black women (but not black men) have a much lower bone loss with age than their white counterparts (only half as great from ages 40 to 80). Although dietary and female hormonal deficiencies have been proposed as causes for such bone loss, neither calcium nor estrogen replacement therapy have proved effective in reversing or delaying these changes in bones.

Bone Disease Related to Age

It has been estimated that clinically identifiable osteoporosis occurs in 10 percent of the persons over 50 years of age (more than 10 million people). Other less common diseases of the skeleton related to age are Paget's disease and degenerative spinal disease, such as spinal disc degeneration. Back pains are the most common and distressing or even debilitating effects of such conditions.

Muscle

As indicated earlier, one universal characteristic of old age is the gradual loss in vigor and speed of muscular movement. Underlying these changes in muscular strength and motor ability are well-documented age-related changes in the structural and physiological properties of muscle.

Structural Changes with Age

As a postmitotic tissue, muscle fibers are incapable of self-replacement after degenerative loss. Accordingly, the most conspicuous degenerative change with age is the progressive loss of muscle mass. This is due to diminution both in diameter and in number of muscle fibers (Gutmann 1977). However, these changes vary in degree depending on the muscles involved and their degree of use as one grows older. Progressive reduction in physical activity is, accordingly, a significant contributory factor in age-related atrophy of skeletal muscle. As muscle fibers atrophy, they are replaced by the increased fat and collagen contents of skeletal muscle. In addition, there is a progressive development and increase in lipofuscin pigment granules in aging muscle.

Degeneration of skeletal muscle often results from damage to and atrophy of nerve fibers innervating the muscle in question. Accordingly, strokes (*cerebrovascular accidents*), which are more common in older persons, may sometimes produce extreme atrophy of limb muscles. As in the case of all motor nerve damage, early physiotherapy can minimize atrophy related to disuse. On the other hand, the gradual, "normal" age-related loss of nerve fibers (see Chapter 5) may also account in part for age losses in muscle fibers. At the level of molecular structure, most enzymes studied (mostly in lower animals) show a decline in activity with age. This is especially true for those enzymes concerned with the release of energy during muscle contraction (Rockstein 1979).

Functional Changes with Age

The progressive loss in muscle strength and speed of movement is a universal manifestation of age in both humans and lower animals. In a number of human muscles, there is a linear decrease in muscle strength from age 30 onward that affects the right-hand grip and the strength of the biceps, wrist, or back muscles. Comparable changes in the force and rate of heart muscle contraction (discussed in Chapter 6) result in a progressive decrease with age in the output of the heart. Fatigue and increased flaccidity (lack of tone) of skeletal muscle also develop in older persons. Impaired muscle coordination, a result of any or all of the above changes, may account for the increased incidence of accidents in older persons.

Muscle Disorders in the Elderly

Many impairments of normal muscle function in the elderly can be related to neurological disorders whose discussion is beyond the scope of this book. Examples are **myasthenia gravis, Parkinsonism,** senile tremor, and senile disorders of gait. (See Freeman 1965 for further details.) Muscular rigidity *(spasticity)* may also result from other causes, as in the case of *hemiplegia* following a stroke.

Summary

Characteristic age changes in the skin are drying, wrinkling, sagging, and, in some persons, the increasing appearance of pigment plaques. The number of sweat glands and production of sweat progressively diminishes. Wound healing becomes slower. The hair progressively thins and grays. Nail growth slows and nails become increasingly dull, opaque, and brittle.

The single authentic aging characteristic of bone is its tendency to diminish in mass. It becomes more brittle and increasingly subject to fracture. This bone loss affects women more than men and white women more than black women. Such progressive bone loss with age is not reversible by either calcium or estrogen supplementation. Degenerative diseases of the spine are much more likely to occur in older persons.

Declining speed and vigor of muscle contraction is a universal manifestation of the aging process in all animals including humans. The primary structural basis for functional deterioration of aging muscle is the gradual, progressive loss in total muscle mass, including both fiber number and size. Secondary bases for failing motor function in aging persons include the "normal" aging of nerves supplying the skeletal muscle and neurological disorders more common in older persons, such as Parkinsonism and stroke.

References

Bertolini, A. M. 1969. Gerontologic metabolism. Charles C. Thomas, Springfield, Ill., pp. 463–504.

Freeman, J. T., ed. 1965. Clinical features of the older patient. Charles C. Thomas, Springfield, Ill., pp. 233–244.

Garn, S. M. 1975. Bone-loss and aging. Pages 39–57 *in* R. Goldman, M. Rockstein, and M. Sussman, eds., The physiology and pathology of human aging. Academic Press, New York.

Gutmann, E. 1977. Muscle. Pages 445–469 *in* C. E. Finch and L. Hayflick, eds., Handbook of the biology of aging. Van Nostrand Reinhold, New York.

Lutwak, L. 1971. Metabolic disorders of the skeleton in aging. Pages 172–179 *in* A. B. Chinn, ed., Working with Older People. IV. Clinical Aspects of Aging. U.S. Dept. of Health, Education and Welfare 1459IV, Rockville, Md.

Montagna, W. 1965. Advances in the biology of the skin. VI. Aging. Pergamon Press, Oxford, pp.1–16.

Rockstein, M. 1979. Muscular changes in aging. *In* C. J. Toga, K. Nandy, and H. Chauncey, eds. Geriatric patients: Dentistry's growing challenge. Lexington Press, Lexington, Mass.

Selmanowitz, V. J., R. L. Rizer, and N. Orentreich. 1977. Aging of the skin and its appendages. Pages 496–509 *in* C. E. Finch and L. Hayflick, eds., Handbook of the biology of aging. Van Nostrand Reinhold, New York.

Chapter Twelve

The Endocrine System

The endocrine system, like the nervous system, is involved in effecting very rapid responses of the body to the changing environment, but the endocrine system performs this function more slowly. Unlike glands with ducts, the **endocrine** glands release their products, *hormones,* directly into the bloodstream. The hormones then have regulatory effects elsewhere on *target* organs or cells. Their effects are concerned with the maintenance of internal constancy of the body, and, in general, the control of metabolism, growth, and development. In addition, the *adrenal medulla* secretes hormones concerned with a variety of adjustments of the body to emergency situations, resulting in a reaction of either ''flight'' or ''fight.''

This chapter will describe the major endocrine glands, their secretions or hormones, and the roles of these secretions in total body functioning. The effects of aging upon these components and functions of the endocrine system is the subject of the second section of the chapter.

Anatomy and Physiology

The major endocrine organs are the *hypothalamus,* the **pituitary,** the **thyroid** and **parathyroids,** the *adrenal cortex,* the *adrenal medulla,* and the *pancreas* (Fig. 12.1). The **gonads,** or reproductive organs of each sex, are additional endocrine sources, to be discussed in the chapter devoted to the reproductive system (Chapter 13).

The Hypothalamus

This small but very important organ (depicted previously in Chapter 5) has both nervous and endocrine functions. As a nerve center, it coordi-

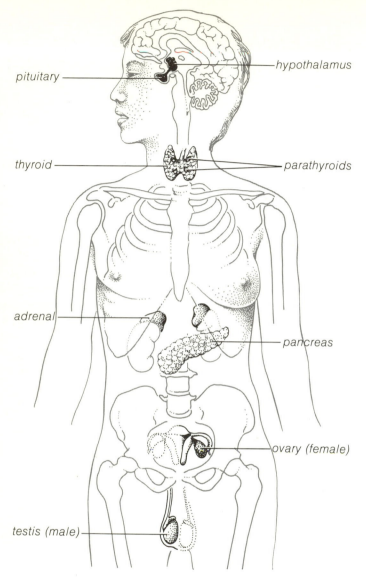

pituitary

hypothalamus

thyroid

parathyroids

adrenal

pancreas

ovary (female)

testis (male)

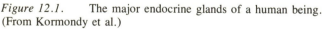

Figure 12.1.   The major endocrine glands of a human being. (From Kormondy et al.)

nates the activities of the autonomic nervous system and is the center of sleep, hunger, thirst, and thermoregulation. As an endocrine gland, it secretes at least 10 polypeptide factors into the blood supply to the pituitary. It controls, in turn, the secretory activities of the pituitary by either stimulating or inhibiting the secretion of **trophic** hormones by the pituitary (see Fig. 12.2).

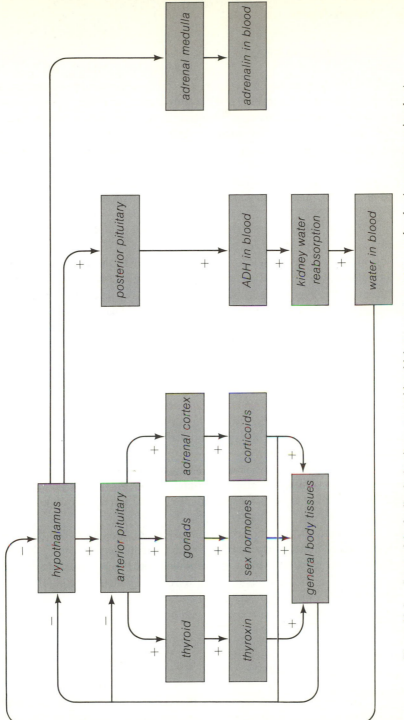

Figure 12.2. Some of the feedback circuits on control in which autonomous nerves and endocrine organs are involved. (From Kormondy et al.)

The Pituitary Gland

Called the master endocrine gland, the pituitary is a pea-sized organ located at the base of the brain near the hypothalamus. It controls the secretory activities of most other endocrine glands as well as cellular metabolism and growth. Its anterior lobe, the **adenohypophysis,** produces (1) *growth hormone* (somatotrophin, GH, or STH), (2) **thyroid-stimulating hormone** (TSH), (3) *adrenocorticotrophic hormone* (ACTH), (4) **luteinizing hormone** (LH, interstitial cell-stimulating hormone, or ICSH), (5) **follicle-stimulating hormone** (FSH), and (6) **prolactin** (lactogenic hormone, luteotrophic hormone, or LTH).

The posterior lobe, the **neurohypophysis,** produces two hormones, **oxytocin** and **vasopressin** (antidiuretic hormone or ADH).

Growth hormone release is effected by GRF, the **growth releasing factor,** and inhibited by GIF, the **growth inhibiting factor,** both of which are produced by the hypothalamus. Growth hormone regulates metabolism and growth of tissues, increasing the rate of protein synthesis. It also influences the cellular metabolism of fats and sugars. In younger persons, it is responsible for the normal growth in size of the limb and other bones and of the soft organs (liver, heart, lungs, kidney, etc.) as the child and adolescent matures. Dwarfism is the result of hyposecretion of GH, and hypersecretion causes gigantism. Hypersecretion in mature persons produces an enlargement of the hands, feet, jaw, and brows known as *acromegaly.*

Prolactin initiates and maintains milk production by the mammary glands. It also stimulates the **corpus luteum** of the ovaries to produce **progesterone** (see Chapter 13).

Oxytocin is secreted in moderate amounts near the end of pregnancy and abundantly at childbirth, effecting contraction of the mother's uterine wall while she is in labor. It is also responsible for active *ejection* of milk in direct response to suckling (see Chapter 13).

Vasopressin, or ADH, controls body water content. When the water content of body fluids is low and the content of solutes (e.g., salts) is high, special volume receptors called the **osmoreceptors** are stimulated in the adenohypophysis. This triggers the release of ADH which acts directly on the kidney tubules to promote water reabsorption and excretion of excess salts into the urine. Conversely, its release is inhibited by high water concentration in body fluids.

The Thyroid Gland

This bilobed gland surrounds the anterior portion of trachea, just adjacent to the larynx. It secretes the hormones **thyroxine** (T_4) and *triiodothyronine* (T3) in direct response to TSH from the adenohypophysis, itself primarily stimulated to do so by **thyroid-releasing factor** from the hypothalamus). High levels of circulating thyroxine in turn exert an inhibitory feedback on secretion of TSH by the pituitary (Fig. 12.2). These two iodine-bearing thyroid hormones stimulate oxygen consumption by the cells, regulate lipid and carbohydrate metabolism, and are necessary for normal growth and tissue differentiation.

The thyroid gland also produces *thyrocalcitonin* which functions like **calcitonin,** the parathyroid hormone (see below).

The Parathyroid Glands

These four tiny glands on the rear surface of the thyroid are responsible for the normal metabolism of calcium and phosphate. When the calcium levels of the blood are reduced, as in the case of dietary deficiency of calcium or vitamin D, parathyroid hormone is released. This in turn causes the removal of calcium and phosphate ions from bone into the *extracellular fluid. Calcitonin,* a second parathyroid hormone, produces the opposite effect. Thus, when the calcium levels of the blood are high, calcitonin is secreted, which results in the rapid deposition of calcium and phosphate into bone. Surgical removal of the thyroid in the case of thyroid tumors or **hyper-thyroidism** usually involves excision of the parathyroids as well. Hormone supplementation is necessary in such cases, or death will follow.

The hormone *thyrocalcitonin* produced by the thyroid gland has a function similar to calcitonin, that is, lowering high calcium levels in the blood.

The Adrenal Glands

The adrenal glands are located just above each kidney on either side of the spinal column. The inner *medulla* secretes the hormones *epinephrine* and *norepinephrine* in situations of emergency and stress. As such, their effects are similar to those produced by the sympathetic division of the autonomic nervous system. The outer portion, the *cortex,* secretes several hormones all classified as *steroids* and referred to collectively as *adrenal corticoids*. These include two important groups, the *mineral corticoids* and the *glucocorticoids* and, in both the male and female, male hormones, or **androgens,** as well. The glucocorticoids, *cortisone* and *cortisol,* are involved in fat and carbohydrate metabolism. They increase blood glucose levels by conversion of non-carbohydrates (like amino acids, glycerol, or lactic acid) to glucose (*gluconeogenesis*). The mineral corticoids, *corticosterone, deoxycorticosterone,* and *aldosterone,* control the electrolyte balance of the blood by promoting reabsorption of sodium and chloride ions by the kidney and increasing potassium excretion. The corticoid androgens are responsible for both male and female **virilism** and sex drive. Precocious puberty in young males with such signs as **hirsutism** (excessive body hair), deepening of the voice, and increased masculine-like muscularity, result from the hypersecretion of these androgens.

Both the glucocorticoids and corticoid androgens are under the control of ACTH secreted by the anterior pituitary. Under conditions of stress (injury, fear, anxiety), the hypothalamus releases CRF (corticotrophin-releasing factor) that in turn stimulates greater ACTH secretion by the anterior pituitary.

The Pancreas

In addition to its exocrine secretions, digestive enzymes released into the small intestine, the pancreas serves as an endocrine gland as well. The endocrine tissue, the islets of Langerhans, consists of two kinds of cells. The alpha cells secrete *glucagon,* and the beta cells, *insulin.* Insulin enhances glucose transfer into cells, whereas glucagon has the opposite effect. Thus as glucose accumulates in the blood, insulin is released to effect its uptake by cells. Glucagon promotes *glycogenolysis,* the release of glucose from stored glycogen in the liver and other cells. Its interaction with insulin maintains blood glucose at normal levels.

Aging of the Endocrine Glands

The Pituitary Gland

Anatomical changes in the pituitary include a significant decrease in its blood supply by age 60, the slow decline beginning at puberty. Its cells become less loosely packed and contain increasing numbers of vacuoles, enlarged **mitochondria,** and irregular outlines of nuclear membranes. The weight of the anterior pituitary decreases after age 50 but to a greater extent in women than in men.

The relationship to the function of the pituitary of these structural changes of aging is not clear. However, there is little decrease in total pituitary content of growth hormone, although the circulating levels do decrease with age between 20 to 39 and 40 to 59 years of age. Yet in obese women, there is no difference in hormone levels between women 20 to 39 years old and 40 to 59 years old. Both TSH and ACTH do not appear to change greatly with age. Similarly, in women, although the gonadotropins increase at puberty, they remain fairly constant throughout the female reproductive years except for fluctuations during the monthly cycle. FSH rises for 15 to 20 years following **menopause** and then declines slowly. LH decreases slowly and LTH disappears completely during the same postmenopause period. (See Bourne 1967, McGavack 1971, and Andres and Tobin 1977 for reviews on aging of the pituitary.)

The Thyroid Gland

Distinct degenerative structural changes take place in the thyroid with advancing age. These include irreversible changes in the cells and replacement of normal connective tissue fibers with dense collagenous fibers. However, comparable functional changes are less evident because, despite a steady decrease in iodine accumulation in the thyroid and in thyroid hormone production with age (beginning at age 35), concomitant reduction in physical activity and basal metabolism likewise occurs. Accordingly, in most older persons the thyroid continues to function adequately and to maintain its reserve capacity. (See Gregerman and Bierman 1974 for an extensive review of age-related changes in the thyroid gland.)

The Parathyroid Glands

The weight of the parathyroid glands increases from infancy up to 30 years of age in men and up to 50 in women. Relatively constant in weight thereafter, they show no significant signs of regression in older persons. Likewise, the secretions of the parathyroid glands remain relatively constant, but can be influenced by both plasma calcium levels and by age changes in the other endocrine glands with which they interact (e.g., the thyroid and adrenal cortex).

The Adrenal Glands

Structural changes in the adrenal glands with age include an increase in pigment accumulation and changes in its characteristic lipid content. Connective tissue, especially collagenous fibers, replaces degenerative cells of the interior and the thickening capsule as well. Vascular dilation and, secondarily, hemorrhage occur in both the cortex and medulla.

Although little is known about functional changes in the medulla with age, both cortisol and corticoid androgen secretions diminish with age. These changes may be the result of both decreased ACTH production by the pituitary and decreased thyroxine production, which has an indirect effect on corticol secretion. There is also some evidence that the cortex is *less sensitive* to ACTH stimulation with age. Aldosterone secretion shows little change with age. Thus, normal salt and water balance tends to be maintained in otherwise healthy old persons. The functional significance of the decrease in secretion of corticoid androgens with age is not clear.

The Pancreas

As in the case of other endocrine glands, it is difficult to assess the functional significance of age-related degenerative structural changes in the pancreas. Progressive degeneration of the beta cells does result in decreasing levels of insulin secretion with advancing age. Correspondingly, as Andres (see Gitman 1967) has pointed out, a reduced glucose tolerance test reaction is evident in at least 50 percent of persons over 65. Yet overt clinical signs and symptoms of *diabetes mellitus* occurs in only 7 percent of such persons, in contrast to only 1 percent of *all* persons under 65. Most adult diabetics, however, do begin to show signs of the disease as early as the age of 40.

Diabetes mellitus.   Diabetes mellitus is the most prevalent *metabolic* disease of old persons. It is due primarily to the failure of the pancreas to secrete adequate levels of insulin. It may, secondarily, result from decreased sensitivity of the various target cells to insulin action. Its signs and symptoms include high levels of glucose in the blood and urine and excessive thirst and urine flow. The breath of the diabetic has an acetone-like smell resembling nail polish remover. This is due to the accumulation of *ketones,* substances that result from the incomplete metabolism of fats, which must be metabolized because of the diminished availability of sugars like glucose for cell metabolism. The ketones and acetoacetic acid resulting from such necessary metabolism of fats leads to *metabolic acidosis,* an acid condition of the blood, in prolonged, uncorrected sieges of diabetes. Chronic untreated diabetes also results in impaired peripheral circulation, leading to gangrene of the toes, fingers, and ultimately the limbs, and to skin ulcers. Other longterm effects include a pronounced loss in body weight as protein stores of muscle as well as fats are utilized as energy sources, circulatory disease of the retina and even blindness, a variety of nervous disorders involving reflexes and gait, and kidney damage. Statistically, diabetes mellitus shows a familial (genetic) distribution and appears to occur to a greater extent in aging *obese* persons.

Summary

As with other organ systems, normal aging of the endocrines is difficult to distinguish from pathological aging. The pituitary gland shows little change in its growth hormone content with advancing age, but the *circulating levels* of this hormone in the blood are reduced among the elderly. Both plasma TSH and ACTH show no change after maturity, remaining constant in old persons. Gonadotropic FSH increases for about two decades after menopause and then declines slowly. LH decreases gradually after menopause.

Thyroid hormone production decreases after age 35. Parathyroid hormone is not influenced by age, but the action of this hormone decreases with age in relation to the observed decline in thyroid activity. Although pancreatic function is difficult to assess, the incidence of diabetes mellitus does increase with age. Cortisol, produced by the adrenal cortex, and adrenal androgens decrease in older individuals. Aldosterone secretion shows little change with age.

References

Andres, R., and J. D. Tobin. 1977. Endocrine system. Pages 357–378 *in* L. Hayflick and C. E. Finch, eds., The handbook of the biology of aging. Van Nostrand Reinhold, New York.

Block, E. 1952. A quantitative morphological investigation of the follicular system in women. Variations at different ages. Acta Anatomica 14:108–123.

Bourne, G. H. 1967. Age changes in the endocrines. Pages 66–75 *in* L. Gitman, ed., Endocrines and aging. Charles C. Thomas, Springfield, Ill.

Gitman, L. 1967. Endocrines and aging. Charles C. Thomas, Springfield, Ill., 305 pp.

Gregerman, R. I., and E. L. Bierman. 1974. Aging and hormones. Pages 1059–1070 *in* R. H. Williams, ed., Textbook of endocrinology. W. B. Saunders, Philadelphia.

McGavack, T. H. 1971. The endocrine system. Pages 194–216 *in* A. B. Chinn, ed., Working with older people. IV. Clinical aspects of aging. U.S. Dept. of Health, Education and Welfare 1459 IV. Rockville, Md.

Talbert, G. B. 1977. Aging of the reproductive system. Pages 318–356 *in* L. Hayflick and C. E. Finch, eds., The handbook of the biology of aging. Van Nostrand Reinhold, New York.

Chapter Thirteen

The Reproductive System

Aging of the reproductive system is of particular concern to the older man and woman from both a biological and an emotional or psychological standpoint. A woman may suffer physical discomfort during and after menopause and may anticipate adverse postmenopausal changes in her femininity. Some women tend to equate the loss of fertility with the likely loss of **libido** and sex appeal. To men, the (often imagined) **climacteric** may seem synonymous with possible impotence and a "loss of manhood." Worry on the part of a postmenopausal woman or a middle-aged man may itself make sexual performance difficult.

This chapter will review the anatomy and physiology of the female and male reproductive systems, with emphasis on the important endocrine functions of these systems. How aging affects the structure and function of the reproductive organs, the endocrine functions, and fertility in both sexes is discussed in the final sections of the chapter. The subject of the changes in sexual response and activity in the older person will be discussed in greater detail in Chapter 14.

Anatomy and Physiology

The female reproductive system includes the *ovaries,* in which the eggs or **ova** develop, the *fallopian tubes* that conduct the eggs from the ovaries to the *uterus,* in which the embryo develops, the external **genitalia,** and the accessory sex organs, the *mammary glands* (Fig. 13.1). The reproductive organs have endocrine functions concerned with the **menstrual cycle,** fetal development, childbirth and lactation, and secondary female sex characteristics.

The male reproductive system includes the paired *testes* that contain the **seminiferous tubules** which produce the **spermatozoa** and the *Leydig's*

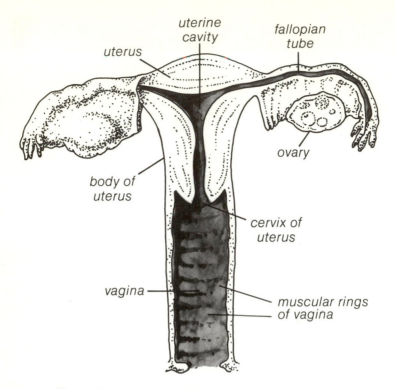

Figure 13.1.   The human female reproductive system.

cells which produce the male sex hormones, the *androgens,* plus small amounts of *estrogens* (Fig. 13.2). The paired spermatic ducts (*vas deferens*) carry the spermatozoa to the *ejaculatory duct* in the **seminal fluid,** which also contains the combined secretions of the *prostate,* the *seminal vesicles,* and the *bulbo-urethral glands.* This duct empties into the *urethra* in the external penis. Thus, the urethra has a combined urogenital function in the male.

Endocrine Functions

The Gonads

As discussed in Chapter 12, the secretion of the hormones of the *gonads* of both males (the testes) and females (the ovaries) is controlled by luteinizing hormone (LH) and follicle-stimulating hormone (FSH), which are secreted by the anterior pituitary, the adenohypophysis.

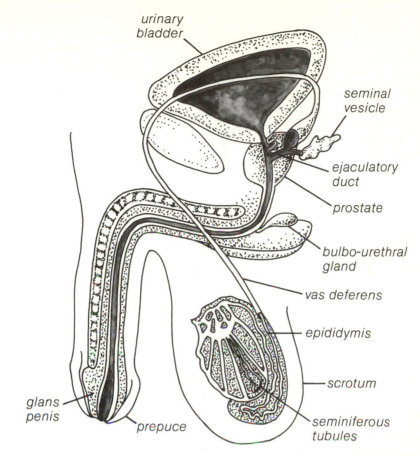

Figure 13.2.   The reproductive system of the human male.

The Testes.   The Leydig's cells of the testes are stimulated by LH to produce large amounts of the androgen **testosterone** and small amounts of estrogens. Sperm production in the seminiferous tubules is dependent on both LH and FSH. Testosterone is responsible for the development and maintenance of the secondary male sex characteristics (body hair, heavier muscularization, development of the external genitalia, and deep voice). By negative feedback, it reciprocally inhibits LH production if its own levels are high. Androgens accelerate growth and promote the retention of sodium, calcium, phosphate, and water. They are also responsible for cessation of bone growth by closing off the growing portions of the bones, the **epiphyses.** Low testosterone production results in more effeminate characteristics, including a more feminine form, a high-pitched voice, and sparser hair.

The Ovaries.   The ovaries produce large amounts of estrogens (*estrone, estriol,* and *estradiol*) and small amounts of the androgen *androstenedione.* Among several other functions, the estrogens are responsible for the growth of the ovarian *follicles* in which the ova develop and for the postpubertal enlargement of the breasts. Their adequate production, in relation to androgen production, is responsible for the secondary female sex characteristics of sparser body hair, high-pitched voice, slender form, and modest muscularization. They are also involved in general metabolism and in closure of the epiphyses, as are the androgens. The ovaries also produce progesterone that, together with the estrogens, helps prepare the **endometrium** (lining) of the uterus for the fertilized ovum.

The Menstrual Cycle

Beginning at puberty (10 to 14 years of age) and usually ending between the ages of 45 to 55 (*menopause*), the *menstrual cycle* is a series of changes recurring in the female sex organs approximately every 28 days. The cycle involves a periodic thickening and vascularization of the capillary-rich endometrium while the ovum is maturing in the *follicle* of the ovary. During this period, estrogen and progesterone levels are elevated. Following ovulation, which is stimulated by LH, and in the absence of fertilization and egg implantation, the endometrium is sloughed off and menstruation occurs. Following an average of 3 to 5 days of the menstrual period, FSH and LH levels rise, inducing maturation of the follicle and its development. The release of these hormones by the adenohypophysis is inhibited by high levels of estrogen and progesterone which suppress the releasing factors for both FSH and LH (Fig. 13.3).

Aging of the Female Reproductive System

The Ovaries and Other Organs

The number of **oocytes** (immature ova) in the human ovary is highest at birth. It decreases markedly thereafter from 700,000 per ovary at birth to 389,300 at puberty to 161,800 by 18 to 24 years of age. At menopause there are only about 11,000 oocytes. At the same time, the number of ova with the normal number of chromosomes declines as well. Children born late in a woman's reproductive life may be abnormal because of such chromosomal abnormalities.

The *fallopian tubes* and *uterine wall* atrophy in old age. The *cervix* and inner cervical epithelium likewise atrophy with advancing age, so that narrowing of the cervical canal may occur.

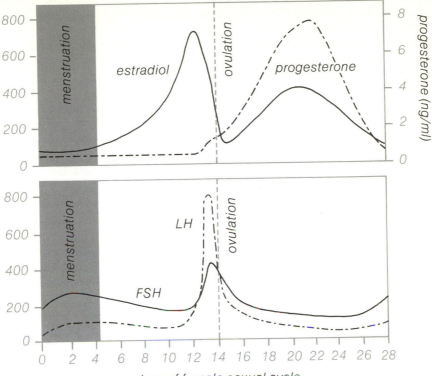

Figure 13.3. Plasma concentrations of the gonadotropins and ovarian hormones during the normal female sexual cycle. (From Guyton, 1976.)

The **vagina** of older postmenopausal women contracts considerably so that it is shorter and the lumen is smaller. The elasticity of the walls of the vagina is markedly reduced due to changes in the elastic fibers in the wall. The epithelium lining the vaginal wall becomes pale, thin, and dry due to reduced circulating estrogen levels which help to maintain the epithelium in youth. The **Bartholin glands,** which normally lubricate the vagina, especially during sexual excitement, become less numerous and less effective in older women. Although the size of the *clitoris* is moderately reduced in aging women, Masters and Johnson (1966) indicate that there is no evidence for loss in its sensate focus.

The most prominent changes in the female reproductive system with age (under hormonal control) occur in the **vulva,** the external genitalia. Both pubic hair and subcutaneous fat are lost. The labial folds flatten, and the skin appears thin, shiny, and pale. Reduced circulating estrogens make the vulva more susceptible to infection and inflammation (*vulvitis*), a common complaint in elderly women. This is even more likely to occur in elderly women with a history of poor hygiene.

As for the body itself there is a decrease in the tone and elasticity of the skin. Mammary glandular tissue is progressively replaced by fat with age, and the breasts may become less firm.

Menopause

As early as the forties, premenopausal women tend to show irregular menses and reduced fertility as the number of egg follicles diminishes through atrophy. The estrogen concentration of the blood decreases with age. Conversely (as would be expected), the blood levels of both LH and FSH reciprocally increase (three and seven times, respectively) from the second decade to menopause. During this premenopausal period, the premenstrual state of the uterus lining becomes less and less fully developed.

Menopause, occurring in the fourth to fifth decade, may last up to two to three years. It is characterized by irregular menses, follicular exhaustion, failure of ova production, and, finally, the permanent cessation of menstrual activity. Some women experience so-called hot flashes during menopause, which are characterized by transitory or brief feelings of being overheated, sweating, and patchy redness beginning in the chest region and extending upward to the neck and face. These symptoms are related to periodic dilations of the finer blood vessels of the skin. In some *postmenopausal* women who receive no estrogen supplementation, the uterus, cervix, and external genitalia begin to undergo the regressive changes detailed above beginning at age 60.

Cancer

Although relatively low compared to other pathologies, cancer of all of the female sexual organs does show increasing incidence with age, especially during and after menopause. Breast cancer shows a dramatic rise in incidence beginning at menopause (from 149 per 100,000 at 45 to 50 years to 200 per 100,000 women at age 70). Breast cancer has an incidence twice that of ovarian cancer at ages 45 to 54, increasing to more than three times that of ovarian cancer at ages 75 to 84. However, chances of *survival* from breast cancer are 20 percent greater than from ovarian cancer at any age.

Aging of the Male Reproductive System

The Testes

About 90 percent of the sperm-producing tubules in the testes are functional in men 20 to 39 years old. This figure decreases to only 50 percent at 50 to 70 years and to only 10 percent after 80. Yet despite the reduction in the number of sperm, the percentage of viable spermatozoa is as high as 68.5 percent at 60 to 70 years, 59.5 percent from 70 to 80 years, and 48.0 percent between 80 and 90 years of age. Thus there are records of men in their seventies, eighties, and, in one case, a 94-year-old man fathering a child.

The circulating level of testosterone, the testicular androgen, changes little until after age 60 (Table 13.1). Thus, in the eighth decade, it has fallen to 40 percent of the circulating level of a mature to middle-aged man.

Auxiliary Reproductive Organs

Histologically, the prostate, seminal vesicles, and bulbo-urethral glands all show age-related regressive changes, especially after age 60. These are reflected in the reduction in volume of the seminal fluid.

The Prostate.   Because of its tendency to show hypertrophy, chiefly **benign** but also malignant, in men past 50, age changes of this organ are well documented. The weight of the prostate increases by about 40 percent by the fifties to sixties, and by 100 percent (double in weight) by the seventh to eighth decades. The epithelial cells of its lining gradually change beginning at age 40. After age 60, these progressive changes seriously reduce secretory activity. At the same time, the smooth muscle involved in the release of its secretions during orgasmic ejaculation diminishes with age and is replaced by dense collagenous fibers. Both benign and malignant prostate hypertrophy may require surgery, because of the effect on the bladder which results in difficulty in urination.

The Penis.   Involutionary changes occur in the *penis* beginning during the third to fourth decades. Sclerosis of both the arteries and veins occurs at this time. The erectile tissue *(corpora cavernosa)* also shows sclerotic changes at this age that become much more generalized in men 55 to 60 years of age. It has been suggested that sexual impotence involving failure of erection in older men may be related to this progressive sclerosis in both the penile blood vessels and erectile tissue.

Table 13.1   Plasma Testosterone Levels

Age (years)	ng./100 ml. plasma
20–50	633 ±25
50–60	582 ±62
60–70	462 ±70
70–80	373 ±46
80–90	245 ±26

Source: Adapted from Talbert 1977.

Summary

Fertility in women begins to decline during the premenopausal period and terminates at menopause; ie., the late fourth to late fifth decades. The number of eggs, maximal at birth, declines steadily to a minimum at premenopause. This is accompanied by decreasing blood levels of estrogens beginning at the second decade, with reciprocal, increased levels of adenohypophyseal LH and FSH. During the early premenopausal but, nevertheless, still reproductive years, the number of abnormal ova and, therefore, abnormal offspring increase with advancing age. Externally the skin and body form become less firm, and mammary glandular tissue becomes progressively replaced by fat. The risk of breast cancer increases with age.

In the aging male, there is a slow but steady decline in the number of sperm-producing (semeniferous) tubules in the testes. Nevertheless, although sperm production correspondingly falls, the percentage of viable spermatozoa remains fairly high even into the seventies. Circulating blood levels of testicular androgens (like testosterone) show little change until after the sixth decade. However, male accessory sex organs all show age changes. The prostate gland particularly undergoes both degenerative cellular changes and (usually benign) hypertrophy. Cancer of the prostate is, likewise, a disease of older men. These regressive changes in the accessory sex organs particularly may be responsible, in part, for sexual inadequacy in some older men.

Involutionary changes both in the veins and arteries and the erectile tissue of the penis may make it increasingly difficult for the older male to achieve and maintain erection.

Nevertheless, as discussed in Chapter 14, in spite of these structural and functional changes, sexual competency *can* and *should* continue into old age for both sexes.

References

Birnbaum, S. J. 1971. Geriatric gynecology. Pages 149–155 *in* A. B. Chinn, ed., Working with older people. IV. Clinical Aspects of Aging. U.S. Dept. of Health, Education and Welfare 1459IV. Rockville, Md.

Block, E. 1952. A quantitative morphological study of the follicular system. Variation at different ages. Acta Anatomica 14:108–123.

Guyton, A. C. 1976. Textbook of medical physiology. W. B. Saunders, Philadelphia, p. 1087.

Masters, W. H., and V. E. Johnson. 1966. Human sexual response. Little, Brown and Co., Boston, pp. 223–241.

Talbert, G. B. 1977. Aging of the reproductive system. Pages 318–356 *in* L. Hayflick and C. E. Finch, eds., Handbook of the biology of aging. Van Nostrand Reinhold, New York.

Chapter Fourteen

Sexual Competency and Aging

Although sexual interest and activity does decline along with aging of the reproductive system, the notion that older people cannot or do not enjoy sexual relations is completely inaccurate. In Chapter 13, aging of the reproductive system was discussed. In this chapter, the several phases of the normal human sexual response will be described first. Changes in both sexual response and sexual activity that accompany aging will then be considered, both in relation to biological aging and to other equally important influences. The effects of such changes in sexual response and sexual activity on the older person's emotional, psychological and sociological well-being will be discussed as well.

Normal Human Sexual Response

The classic studies of Masters and Johnson (1966, 1970) provide a detailed and explicit description of sexual responses of men and women of various age groups. They established that the progressive physiological reaction to sexual stimuli for both sexes includes (1) the excitement phase, (2) the plateau phase, (3) the orgasmic phase, and (4) the resolution phase. The duration and intensity of the entire cycle or any of its four phases depend upon a broad spectrum of factors. These include parental conditioning and other prior experiences, socioethical standards of one's social stratum, and the conditions surrounding the particular sexual experience. The combined observations of over 600 men and women, however, yielded the description of each of the phases of the total sexual response summarized below.

The Excitement Phase. This first phase may develop from either *somatogenic* (tactile, visual, auditory, or olfactory) stimuli or *psychogenic* (fantasy or dream) stimuli. If sufficiently prolonged and intense, it will extend into the next phase. Erection of the penis in the male and preparation of the vaginal canal in the female for containment before and during orgasm particularly mark this period.

The Plateau Phase.   Sexual tension is reinforced and heightened during this period. Likewise penile and vaginal changes continue progressively to a point where orgasm can be achieved. In women, elevation of the uterus (in apparent preparation for receiving the ejaculate) also occurs during this phase.

The Orgasmic Phase.   This phase is of very brief duration, usually a matter of seconds. It is the point, for a particular sexual incident, where maximal sexual tension in the sexual act occurs. In men, it is climaxed by ejaculation of the semen from the penis (via the urethra). It is accomplished by three or four rapid, major expulsive efforts occurring at approximately 0.8-second intervals. Orgasm in women involves three to five or as many as ten or even fifteen successive contractions of the vagina, also occurring at rapid-fire 0.8-second intervals. Uterine contractions may also occur in the female orgasm. In men, subjective awareness of orgasm involves the penis, prostate, and testis and is entirely pelvic in nature. In women, however, it may involve singly the clitoris, the vagina, or the uterus, or any combination of these, depending on individual variations.

The Resolution Phase.   The period of return from the height of sexual climax to a distinct reversal of phases is called the resolution phase. It results in the return of the sexual partner to an unstimulated state. Men exhibit a refractory period during this phase. During this refractory period, restimulation to a second excitement level sufficiently high to produce a second orgasm is not possible. Women, on the other hand, have the potential to return to one or more orgasmic phases from *any point* in the resolution phase and therefore experience multiple orgasms.

Age Changes in Sexual Response

Aging Women

Observations of women ranging from 40 to 75 years of age have definitely established that there is no limit, as to age, to human female sexual activity. Physiologically, women have the capacity for successful, normal sexual activity well into extreme old age for which the only prerequisites are good health, a positive attitude, and an effective sexual partner. Thus, the healthy aging woman normally has sex drives that demand resolution. Despite the known changes in the various sex and reproductive organs occurring before, during, and after menopause, older women continue to experience the four phases of sexual response (even at 60 and 70 years of age). Failure to do so may be due to physical, cultural, sociological, or psychological factors.

The Excitement Phase.   Normally involving 15 to 30 *seconds* in younger women, this phase may be prolonged to as long as 5 *minutes* before the plateau phase is reached in sexually active women from 40 to 70. Incidence and intensity of such responses as nipple erection, tumescence of breasts and of the vaginal glands and of the labia minora, as well as vaginal lubrication, are progressively reduced after age 40.

The Plateau Phase.   Intensity of response, including enlargement of the nipple areas and elevation of the uterus, is somewhat reduced with age.

The Orgasmic Phase.   The onset of orgasm in older women may be fairly rapid, although its duration is considerably reduced from 50 to 70 years of age. Vaginal contractions are reduced in number from five to ten in women 20 to 30 years old to as few as three to five in still sexually active postmenopausal females. Uterine contractions tend to be spasmodic rather than rhythmic with senile involution of the uterus (Chapter 13). Moreover, where uterine contractions do occur they may be accompanied by severe cramping pain.

The Resolution Phase.   Most women after age 50 retain obvious nipple erection up to hours after orgasm. However, virtually all other changes in the genitalia and internal organs associated with sexual performance return to the nonstimulated state much more rapidly than in younger women.

Aging Men

If there is indeed a male climacteric, it plays little, if any, role in lessening sexual interest and response in the aging man. This is consistent with the potential of the human male to be sexually functional and even reproductive well into the eighth decade and even beyond in rare cases. Although endocrine changes that accompany the climacteric may be responsible in part for the diminishing sexual response in the aging man, impotence is more likely to have psychological rather than physiological causes. One aspect of male sexuality which normally does not change with age is the ability to achieve and maintain erection during *coitus* (intercourse). In general, how-ever, the *intensity* of male sexual response is reduced with advancing age.

Excitement Phase.   Although the ability to achieve erection con-tinues well into advanced old age, the time required to do so increases about two or three times, from the average of 3 to 5 seconds in young men to 10 or more seconds in older men.

Plateau Phase.   The plateau phase is prolonged in older men, so that there is a greater capacity to sustain erection without ejaculation for much longer periods of time. This capacity, however, may increase the effectiveness of the older man as a sexual partner since many women require a prolonged excitement or plateau phase to reach orgasm.

The Orgasmic Phase.   By contrast, climax in older men is of considerably shorter duration. Ejaculation in men over 60 is complete in one to two rather than three or four expulsive contractions observed in younger men. Expulsion of ejaculatory jets in men over 60 is reduced to half the distance (1 to 2 feet) for young men. The ejaculate becomes scantier and thinner.

Resolution Phase.   Loss of erection and return to penile flaccidity occurs in seconds in men over 60 in contrast to minutes or even hours in younger males (12 to 24 hours in some cases).

Age Changes in Sexual Activity

Kinsey and coworkers (1948, 1953) originally reported that a person's sexual habits in later years are essentially a continuation of his or her earlier sexual habits. Thus people who are sexually active in younger years will continue to be so in old age. This may be reinforced by renewed inter-dependence of husband and wife with the departure of children from the home, financial security, and continued good health. Nevertheless, whereas young married couples engage in coitus about four to five times per week, this frequency usually diminishes with time. Couples at age 50 report having intercourse an average of 1.8 times per week. Even in the absence of chronic debilitating illness, many contributory negative factors may affect sexual habits. The most important factor is the availability of a suitable mate, which affects women more than men, especially after age 70, because of the higher male mortality rate.

Aging Women

Although decreasing endocrine levels have an influence on sexual activity in older women, psychological or social factors may be even more important in the greater age-related reduction in female than in male sexual activity. In women whose upbringing has conditioned them to identify sex with reproduction, sexual interest may cease with the climacteric. For the older woman who has previously experienced both regular and satisfying sexual activity, the decreasing availability of a male sex partner make fulfillment of the sexual drive difficult. In addition, despite changing mores and the increasing number of relationships between older women and younger men, such associations are more often ridiculed than applauded. However, such relationships are becoming more common due in part to the increasing popularity of facial and even body, surgical "rejuvenation."

For some women, on the other hand, the termination of the fear of pregnancy by menopause makes sexual activity all the more attractive; as indicated earlier, there are no *physiological* reasons why regular female sexual activity cannot continue well into advanced postmenopausal years. In fact, the 1966 Duke Study found that older married women showed a high sustained and often rising interest in and frequency of sexual activity (Verwoerdt, Pfeiffer, and Wang 1966). However, 95 to 96 percent of unmarried women over 60 reported *no* sexual activity at all.

Aging Men

As in the case of women, there is a steady sharp drop in both sexual interest and activity in men with advancing age despite the increasing ratio of women to men. The primary contributing physiological factor is the increased incidence with age of chronic disabling illnesses, which is higher in men than in women. However, the inability to perform sexually (impotence) despite continued sexual *interest* usually indicates a psychological rather than a physiological problem. Such problems may include boredom, fear of failure, chronic depression and anxiety, and chronic tension resulting from widowhood, loss of friends, retirement, and fear of dying.

In one study of 74 men aged 64 to 91, 75 percent reported continued sex interest, but only 55 percent experienced actual sexual activity (Freeman 1961). The Duke Study found that, although both married and unmarried aging men showed a steady decline in both sexual *interest* and *activity,* the decline with age in sexual interest was greater for married than for unmarried men. However, both married and unmarried men showed a similar age distribution of declining sexual *activity*. Of the men over age 60, 53 percent reported having sexual intercourse at least once a week. Half of the men over age 75 (50 percent) reported having continuing sexual intercourse. More significantly, 20 percent of the men over 80 (some over 90) reported engaging in sexual activity once a month.

Aging, Disease, and Sexuality

A common concomitant of diabetes in both men and women is sexual dysfunction. In women, the failure to achieve orgasm is accompanied by reduced vaginal lubrication, a common attendant problem in female diabetics. Similarly, 50 percent of the male diabetics studied were incapable of having an erection in heterosexual activity or masturbating. Therefore, for both sexes, sexual impotence accompanying diabetes, a disease more common in older persons, appears to have no effective remedial therapy.

It is an accepted fact that excessive alcohol intake has a depressing effect on sexual activity. Accordingly, the relatively high incidence of alcoholism in persons over 65 contributes to the reduced sexual interest and potency in that age group. Similarly, the increased regular use of drugs by older persons, who suffer from chronic diseases to a greater extent than all younger age groups, often diminishes sexual interest and competency. Tranquilizers, antidepressant drugs, or the interaction of several drugs being taken concomitantly for several ailments can have adverse effects.

Psychological and Emotional Implications of Sexual Aging

The pioneer studies of Kinsey and coworkers (1948, 1953) and of Masters and Johnson (1966) have done much to minimize the sexual taboos which the culture of civilized persons has established. Along with those of Butler and Lewis (1976), they have also served to dispel many completely mistaken notions concerning sexuality in later years, revealing that older people have not only the ability to perform sexually but, more importantly, the ability to enjoy sexual relations very late in life.

However, even more importantly, these studies stress the psychological and emotional importance of sexual activity as part of a normal, healthy existence at any age. As Ruth Weg (1975) has so effectively stated the case, since nature has provided women the capacity for continuing sexual activity long after their procreative ability ceases, the physical act of coitus must serve not only a procreational purpose but also that of mutual emotional satisfaction and personal realization. Thus this most intimate kind of interpersonal communication satisfies the basic human needs of mutual desire, love, intimacy, and recognition in both men and women. Continued acceptance as a sex partner represents an expression of all of these important man-woman relationships to older men and women in the later, golden years of their lives.

Summary

Sexual interest and activity in women can extend well beyond the onset of the postreproductive period, the menopause. The capacity for sexual response extends well into the seventies, with some diminution in intensity and a prolongation of the first two (excitation and plateau) phases of the sexual act. Similarly, the healthy aging male is capable of sexual arousal and performance well into the eighties. Of all aspects of the sexual act, the ability to achieve and maintain erection during coitus does not change with age. However, a longer duration of the excitement and plateau phases, a diminished intensity and duration of orgasm (ejaculation), and rapid resolution (loss of erection) are characteristic of the sexual response of older men.

Sexual habits in later life are, in general, a reflection of one's habits in earlier years. Nevertheless, whereas young married couples may engage in coitus an average of four to five times per week, this falls to less than two times per week at age 50. Numerous factors affect the frequency of sexual activity in old age. These include the availability of an appropriate sex partner, health, and psychological factors such as boredom, postmenopausal insecurity, postretirement depression and anxiety, or fear of death.

In the female, postmenopause endocrine starvation and accompanying structural changes in the sexual organs may discourage or reduce the frequency and effectiveness of the sexual act. Cultural taboos arising from the concept that the sex act is purely procreative in nature may also discourage sexual activity or interfere with successful performance. On the other hand, freedom from the fear of pregnancy may enhance the interest and level of sexual response, particularly in the married postmenopausal woman.

The average healthy aging male similarly shows diminished frequency of sexual activity with advancing age. The cause of impotence is most often psychological rather than physiological in otherwise healthy men of *any* age. Emotional problems following retirement, ranging from reduced income, loss of peer role in business and family, and boredom all may lessen sexual interest and diminish frequency of sexual activity. Nevertheless, some men over 80 report engaging in sexual activity at least once a month.

Continued successful and mutually satisfying sexual activity has profound emotional implications at all ages but especially in older persons. In dealing with men and women of advanced age, the geriatric practitioner, counselor, or social worker must not underestimate the importance of fostering the continuation of this significant interpersonal relationship well into the last decades of life in aging men and women.

References

Butler, R. N., and M. I. Lewis. 1976. Sex after sixty. Harper and Row, New York. 165 pp.

Freeman, J. T. 1961. Sexual capacities in the aging male. Geriatrics 16:37–43.

Hite, S. 1976. The Hite report. Macmillan, New York, pp. 369–383.

Kinsey, A. C., W. B. Pomeroy, and C. E. Martin. 1948. Sexual behavior in the human male. W. B. Saunders, Philadelphia, pp. 218–262.

Kinsey, A. C., W. B. Pomeroy, C. E. Martin, and P. H. Gebhard. 1953. Sexual behavior in the human female. W. B. Saunders, Philadelphia, pp. 132–446.

LeWitter, M., and A. Abarbanel. 1977. Aging and sex. Pages 75–81 *in* A. Ellis and A. Abarbanel, eds., The encyclopedia of sexual behavior. Jason Aronson, New York, pp. 75–81.

Masters, W. H., and V. E. Johnson. 1966. Human sexual response. Little, Brown and Co., Boston, pp. 223–270.

Masters, W. H., and V. E. Johnson. 1970. Human sexual inadequacy. Little, Brown and Co., Boston, pp. 316–350.

Rubin, I. 1965. Sexual life after sixty. Basic Books, New York. 274 pp.

Verwoerdt, A. E., A. E. Pfeiffer, and H. S. Wang. 1969. Sexual behavior in senescence. Geriatrics 14:137–154.

Weg, R. 1975. Sexual inadequacy in the elderly. Pages 203–227 *in* R. Goldman, M. Rockstein, and M. Sussman, eds., The physiology and pathology of human aging. Academic Press, New York.

Biological Aging and Its Implications
Aspects of Retirement
Planning for Retirement
References

Chapter Fifteen

Human Aging:
A Multifaceted Phenomenon

Aging is a lifelong and multifaceted phenomenon. In youth and early adulthood, it normally involves the attainment of maximum physical well-being and, concomitantly, optimal economic and social status. Beginning in late middle age, the detrimental aspects of biological aging become increasingly evident with advancing age.

Throughout this book, the social and psychological implications of the failing function of various organ systems have been stressed wherever appropriate. This chapter will summarize the significant changes in body function and review the mutual interaction of biological, economic, social, and behavioral changes with advancing age. Finally, the effects of retirement on the lives of the elderly and some aspects of planning for retirement will be discussed.

Biological Aging and Its Implications

In external appearance, an old person is someone whose skin is wrinkled, whose hair is gray, and who is bent or stooped and moves slowly. The less conspicuous, internal functional changes with age typically involve a gradual, more or less linear decrement in performance for most of the organ systems of the body.

Failing motor ability, a universal aging phenomenon, involves reduced speed and diminished vigor of muscle contraction, reflecting the gradual decrement in the number of nerve cells and skeletal muscle fibers (the only two postmitotic human tissues). The total effect is an ever-decreasing mobility, secondarily resulting in isolation. Both factors may be accelerated or exacerbated by failing physical or mental health (such as arthritis or heart disease or depression and anxiety). Inability to move about readily may limit one's ability to market and to prepare meals. Malnutrition is quite common in the aged for this as well as for economic and psychological reasons. Reduced mobility also means more limited participation in social activities outside the home, such as attending sports events, the theater, an opera or concert, playing bridge or backgammon with friends, or going to clubs or friends' parties). Thus the older person may become a virtual prisoner in his or her own home, becoming dependent on friends or relatives for transportation. Boredom, depression, or anxiety often result from such social isolation. Psychosomatically, such mental states may affect adversely one's physical health. Gastrointestinal distress and hypertension are conditions that are often emotionally related.

The gradual deterioration with age of the nervous system includes a slowing of reflex responses, poorer muscular coordination, and failing vision. These conditions are responsible in part for the increasing incidence of falls and accidents in aging men and women. Age-related demineralization of bone makes fractures more likely when an older person falls. Secondarily, with the repeated occurrence of such accidents, even if they are not serious, older persons may lose confidence in themselves and become increasingly timid about going out.

Also related to the deterioration of the nervous system is the reduced ability of the body to maintain its normal core temperature. This, in part, may be the cause of the relatively high incidence of respiratory infections that increases with age. The increasing incidence of constipation, the result of reduced intestinal motility, may in turn be related to both the failing of the autonomic nervous system as well as reduced physical activity. Likewise, fecal or urinary incontinence may occur, especially in advanced cases of senile dementia or organic brain syndrome. Incontinence is a serious problem in the home especially to a spouse who may in turn be physically incapable of attending to such a person. Loss of memory, disorientation, confusion, agitation, or paranoia may similarly contribute to the seriousness of the problem of maintaining such mentally ill, older persons in the home. In such cases, funds and facilities permitting, institutionalization may be the only solution.

Faulty vision and hearing are also inevitable consequences of aging of the nervous system. Especially where defective hearing or total deafness remain uncorrected, serious behavioral aberrations may result. The decreased ability to participate in normal activities and the auditory isolation of these people can result in irritability, anxiety, or even mild to severe paranoia.

Extensive studies have shown that sexual competency in humans persists well into the seventh, eighth, or even ninth decades. However, age changes in the skin as well as gradual deteriorative structural changes in the reproductive system (especially in women) represent a common basis for reduced sexual activity in the aging. Surgical "rejuvenation" and the judicious, supervised administration of female sex hormones, may influence the continuation of sexual activity.

The single universally distributed characteristic of biological aging is the increasing loss with age in the body's reserve capacity to recover from displacing environmental changes (especially stress). Thus, there is a diminished tolerance to glucose injection and changing blood acidity and to recovery from exercise-induced elevations of blood pressure, heart rate, and respiratory minute volume. Decrements in kidney function, in basal metabolic rate, and in respiratory functions (maximum breathing capacity) likewise represent a lowered ability of the aging human to resist environmental stresses.

However, it is important to remember that the norms of biological aging that have been discussed in this book, are, at best, statistically defined. Indeed, some 80-year-olds have a total physiological capacity equal to that of the average person one or two decades younger. Similarly, age does not necessarily have the same effect on the different organ systems within one individual nor on the same organ in different persons. Thus, a 75-year-old person may have the cardiac output of an average 60-year-old, whereas renal function may be that of an average person of the same age or older. Accordingly, chronological aging must indeed be considered a myth (Butler 1975) and cannot be equated with biological aging.

Aspects of Retirement

Of all the social aspects of aging, the practice in our society of retirement, usually at age 65, has the broadest implications to the ever-growing population age 65 and over. These implications range from economic privation to changes in social and family status and, very often, adverse psychological effects on the retired person.

First and foremost, a diminished income means a restriction in life style. To the retiree of middle income with a modest retirement income, the inexorable, continued shrinkage of the dollar means attrition of all kinds. One of the biggest problems facing the large population of older persons is the ever-increasing cost of food. Retirees notoriously shift to inadequate and often poorly balanced diets poor in protein and rich in carbohydrates. Malnutrition and lack of vitamins greatly contribute to poor health, especially a greater susceptibility to infectious disease. At the same time, the continually rising costs of health care for a population which spends over three times as much (over $800 per person in 1976) as persons under 65 means an inability to get necessary medical attention. The significance of these facts for an age group that has the highest percentage of *chronic* ailments and respiratory diseases is obvious.

Retirement has additional serious adverse effects on one's role among peers, in the family, and in the community. The abrupt termination of work status usually reduces the factory worker, the teacher, the business executive, or the politician to feeling like just another old person without a role. Likewise a former head of the household may even become dependent on financial assistance from his or her children to live an even highly modified life style. Financial restrictions on social and leisure activities (social club membership, the theater, concert or sporting events, dining out, entertaining, etc.) likewise contribute significantly to lowering the retiree's morale. The resulting social isolation in turn increases further the boredom, apathy, and depression associated with other aspects of retirement.

However, retirement, which occupies about 15 to 20 percent of the average person's life span, affects different persons differently. Broad surveys have shown that persons active in their youth and middle years continue to be active upon retirement. Those who have led a quiet, restricted existence, working at routine, perhaps stultifying jobs, may continue unmotivated, bored, and even self-isolated or withdrawn after retirement. In short, older people are as different as people of any other age group. Some are in better physical or mental health than others. Some have an optimistic outlook on life and are enthusiastic and active whereas others are depressed and apathetic. Yet most older people want to retain their own *individual* identity and do not want to be perceived or treated according to a stereotype based purely on chronological age.

Planning for Retirement

All of the above considerations clearly emphasize the need for a preparation for retirement, preferably beginning in middle age. Just as retirement is multifaceted, so must retirement planning include provision for all of its aspects. Providing adequately for financial needs is probably the most challenging of all retirement problems. Adequate health care, locale of retirement life, and provision for additional activities to replace one's full-time job must be planned for as well.

Aside from Social Security benefits and company pensions, supplemental sources of income are necessary to offset inflation and shrinking purchasing power. Additional sources may be supplemental personal retirement programs or income investments in conservative securities with dividends, income property, or the like. Part-time employment serves the dual purpose of providing income, as well as meeting the need of the retiree to be occupied.

Aside from income, the meaningful use of so much additional leisure time upon retirement is especially important. Developing hobbies and interests and shifting from more strenuous to other sports (including spectator sports) should be included in preretirement planning. To the ambitious person, retirement provides a chance to complete an interrupted education or even to work for an advanced degree, an activity that not only fills time but which may also be highly gratifying. Continuing education may also open new vistas of activity in areas like creative writing, amateur theatrical art, sculpture, and music for an otherwise bored, unoccupied retiree. In many cases, training experience in amateur art, writing, or part-time counseling may lead to income as well as personal satisfaction. Voluntary community service can also be a time-consuming and rewarding occupation. Gray Ladies or Big Brothers, advisors to failing small businesses, and volunteer teacher's aides are examples of opportunities available to the retiree. The Gray Panthers have done much to counteract stereotypes of older people.

The various concomitants of the later years tend to complement one another to some degree. Accordingly, as this book has attempted to emphasize, the practitioner as well as the administrator of services to the elderly must maintain an alertness to the likelihood of complex interaction of biological changes with economic, social, and emotional decrements with advancing age.

References

Butler, R. N. 1975. Why survive? Being old in America. Harper & Row, New York. 496 pp.

Comfort, A. 1976. A good age. Crown Publishers, New York. 224 pp.

Glossary

Adenohypophysis.   The anterior lobe of the pituitary gland that produces several major endocrine hormones.

Afferent nerve.   A nerve that transmits nerve impulses towards the central nervous system from the periphery.

Aging.   Structural and functional changes that occur with passing time in an organism. *See also* Senescence.

Aldehyde.   A class of very reactive organic compounds with a typical structure such as to render it a strong oxidizing agent.

Alpha-tocopherol (vitamin E).   A vitamin found in wheat germ, cotton seed, palm oil, etc., necessary for normal pregnancy in female rats and for preventing sterility in male rats.

Alveoli.   Microscopic sacs in the lungs where oxygen from the air enters the blood and carbon dioxide is expelled from the blood.

Alzheimer's disease.   A form of senile dementia usually occurring in persons *under* 50 years of age and characterized by impaired orientation, judgement, and memory.

Androgen.   Any one of a number of male sex hormones.

Aneurysm.   An abnormal dilation of a blood vessel, particularly an artery, resulting from weakness in some part of its wall.

Antioxidant.   Any chemical substance that inhibits oxidation. (Includes a number of food additives like tocopherols, employed as preservatives.)

Arrhythmia, cardiac.   A variation in the normal rhythm or rate of the heart.

Arteriosclerosis.   The loss of elasticity or hardening of the walls of the arteries.

Arthritis.   A painful condition of the bone joints, usually characterized by inflammation.

Ascorbic acid (vitamin C).   The vitamin needed to prevent bleeding gums (scurvy).

Atheroma.   A fatty plaque or deposit on the inner wall surface (intima) of blood vessels (usually arteries).

Atherosclerosis.   A fibrous thickening of the inner walls (intima) of blood vessels accompanied by the accumulation of soft, pasty, acellular fatty material.

Atrium (*pl.* atria).   The upper thin-walled chamber of the heart that receives blood from the veins returning blood to the heart.

Atrophy.   Wasting away of tissue or organ cells.

Auricle.   See Atrium.

Autoimmunity.   Attack response by the immune system of the body to its own tissues as a result of the production of antibodies against such antigens.

Autonomic nervous system.   That part of the nervous system, consisting of sympathetic and parasympathetic nerves, that carries impulses to organs not primarily under conscious control.

Axon.   A nerve cell process that carries impulses from the cell body to a junction with another cell.

Bartholin glands.   Glands located on either side of the vaginal opening that produce lubricating secretions.

Basal metabolic rate (BMR).   The rate of expenditure of energy under specified conditions of a fasting person under inactive but awake conditions.

Benign.   Of a mild or relatively mild nature, such as benign or noncancerous tumors.

Bile.   A yellowish or greenish viscous fluid containing salts, secreted by the liver and stored in the gall bladder.

Bolus.   A rounded mass; a term usually used to describe a mass of food in the digestive tract.

Bronchi (*sing.* bronchus).   The main branches of the trachea or windpipe that lead to each lung.

Bronchiole.   A smaller branch of the bronchi that terminates in a number of alveoli.

Calcitonin.   A hormone produced by the parathyroid gland involved in the regulation of calcium levels in body fluids.

Calorie.   A unit of heat, equal to that of the heat required to raise the temperature of 1 kilogram of water by 1°C at 22°C.

Cardiac cycle.   One complete two-phase cycle of the heart consisting of contraction (systole) followed by relaxation (diastole).

Cardiology.   The clinical study of the function of the heart and major blood vessels in health and disease.

Cardiomegaly.   Enlargement of the heart.

Carbon dioxide.   A gaseous compound commonly resulting from the complete oxidation of carbon compounds such as fats, starches, and sugars.

Cartilage.   A tough, elastic tissue that composes most of the skeleton in the embryo which, for the most part, is converted in the adult to bone. It is sometimes referred to as gristle.

Central nervous system.   The part of the nervous system that includes the brain and spinal cord.

Cerebellum.   The part of the vertebrate brain which controls muscle coordination.

Cerebrum.   The region of the vertebrate brain, especially large and well developed in mammals, that controls many voluntary functions and is the seat of the higher mental capacities in humans.

Chromosomes.   The structures found within the nucleus of the cell that contain the genes, the hereditary determiners.

Chronic disease.   A disease that persists over a prolonged period of time or is characterized by a slow progression of worsening symptoms.

Cilia.   Very fine thread-like extensions of protoplasm that project from the surfaces of some cells and are capable of wave-like movement.

Climacteric.   The time of middle life when the body undergoes marked, permanent changes. It is usually used to describe menopause, the cessation of the menses, in women.

Colitis.   Inflammation of the large intestine, especially of its mucous membrane.

Collagen.   A protein that is the chief component of connective tissue in general and the organic substance of bone. It is found in fibrous tissue, cartilage, and bone.

Colon.   The large intestine.

Compliance.   A measure of deformability; the ease with which an expandable organ like the lung can be distended.

Constipation.   A bowel condition in which fecal evacuations are infrequent and difficult. In such cases, the large bowel becomes filled with hardened feces.

Corpus leteum.   The reddish-yellow endocrine structure filling the Graafian follicle of the ovary after discharge of the ovum.

Coronary insufficiency.   A difficult-to-diagnose heart condition, characterized by chest pain. There is little evidence of specific heart tissue damage, but the condition is due to impaired coronary vessel blood flow.

Cortex.   The outer layer of a structure such as the cerebral cortex or adrenal cortex.

Cyanocobalamin (vitamin B12).   The antianemia factor of liver extract.

Cytoplasm.   The substance of the cells exclusive of the nucleus and the vacuoles.

Demography.   The statistical study of the incidence or distribution within populations of births, deaths, marriages, diseases, etc.

Dendrite.   A short, usually branched protoplasmic process of the neuron that receives nerve impulses from the axons of other nerve cells and carries them towards the central nerve body.

Dermis.   The deep layer of the skin lying beneath the outer epidermis. It contains the blood vessels of the skin and the sensory receptors.

Diabetes mellitus.   A pathological condition characterized by an excess of sugar in the blood and the excretion of carbohydrates not used by the body in the urine.

Diaphragm.   A flat sheet of fibrous and smooth muscle that separates the thoracic from the abdominal cavity.

Diastole.   The relaxation phase of the heart muscle during the cardiac cycle.

Diastolic pressure.   Arterial blood pressure, measured during diastole (relaxation of the heart) in the cardiac cycle.

Diverticulosis.   An abnormal condition in which a number of diverticula (blind sacs) are present in the walls of the intestine.

DNA (deoxyribonucleic acid).   A high molecular weight compound found primarily in the nuclei of cells, which carries the genetic information necessary for normal functioning of the cells of the organism.

Dyspnea.   Labored or troubled breathing.

Ectopic beat.   A heartbeat originating in a region of the heart other than the normal "pacemaker" region (the sinoatrial node).

Edema.   Swelling caused by outflow of serous fluid into connective tissues, due to defective circulation.

Efferent nerve.   A nerve that carries impulses away from the central nervous system to effector organs like the muscles or glands.

Elastic fibers.   Connective tissues consisting of networks of elastin.

Elastin.   An albumin-like protein, which is the principal component of elastic fibers.

Enzyme.   A protein which acts as a catalyst, accelerating a cellular metabolic reaction.

Embolism.   Blockage of a blood vessel by an embolus.

Embolus (*pl.* emboli).   Any particle blocking the circulation in a blood vessel (e.g., a blood clot).

Emphysema.   A disease in which the walls separating adjacent alveoli breakdown, greatly decreasing the respiratory surface area of the lungs.

Endocardium.   A thin, serous membrane lining the cavities of the heart.

Endocrine (hormone).   A regulatory chemical compound secreted in relatively small amounts by ductless glands into the bloodstream and producing their regulatory effects some distance from their site of origin.

Endometrium.   The mucous membrane that lines the uterus.

Epidermis.   The outer (epithelial) layer of the skin.

Epiphysis.   That part of bone that is formed independently and joined later to complete whole bone.

Esophagus.   The tubular portion of the gastrointestinal tract that carries food from the pharynx to the stomach.

Estrogen.   The generic term for the hormonal substance involved in the female monthly cycle or estrus; the female sex hormone.

Excretion.   The elimination of waste products from the body.

Expiration.   Exhalation of air from the lungs through the nose or mouth.

Extracellular fluid.   The liquid bathing all cells and serving as the medium of exchange (between cells and between cells and capillaries) of nutritive materials and products of metabolic activity.

Fibrillation.   Abnormal arrhythmic contractions or twitchings of the heart muscle.

Fibrosis.   Excessive growth and accumulation of fibrous connective tissue in place of functional tissue in an organ.

Flutter.   Abnormally rapid beating of the heart. In atrial flutter, the upper chambers (atria) of the heart may contract 250 to 400 times a minute.

Follicle-stimulating hormone (FSH).   A hormone secreted by the anterior lobe of the pituitary gland (the adenohypophysis), that stimulates and induces maturation of the follicles of the ovaries and the liberation of estrogen.

Fraternal (heterozygous) twins.   Twins that develop from two different ova; they need not necessarily be of the same sex.

FSH.   *See* Follicle-stimulating hormone.

Gastritis.   Inflammation of the stomach.

Gene.   The basic unit of heredity; each gene has a specific location on a particular chromosome in the nucleus of cells.

Genetic code.   The genetic information carried by specific DNA molecules of chromosomes.

Genitalia.   The male and female external sex organs.

Geriatrics.   The practice of medicine concerned with the diseases associated with old age.

Germ cells.   Those cells in the body, found in the testes and ovaries, that produce the sperm and ova.

Gerontology.   That branch of science concerned with aging.

Geropsychiatry.   That aspect of the practice of psychiatry concerned with the problems of old age.

Glaucoma.   A condition of the eye characterized by a marked increase in intraocular pressure.

Glomerular filtration.   The filtration of plasma through the walls of the coiled capillaries of the tufts of the glomerular tubules into the collecting tubules of the kidneys.

Glycogen.   A complex carbohydrate (polysaccharide) synthesized from glucose, especially in the liver and muscle.

Gonads.   The reproductive glands; the ovaries and testes.

Growth hormone-inhibiting factor (GIF).   A hypothalamic hormone that inhibits the release of growth hormone.

GRF.   *See* Growth hormone-releasing factor.

Growth hormone-releasing factor.   A hormone produced by the hypothalamus that promotes the release of growth hormone from the pituitary.

Heart valves.   Structures situated between the upper and lower chambers (atria and ventricles) of the heart and at the entrance to the pulmonary artery and aorta that prevent the back-flow of blood during systole.

Hirsutism.   The presence of excessive body hair.

Histone.   One of a number of simple proteins containing a high proportion of *basic* amino acids.

Hormone.   *See* Endocrine.

Hyaline.   A term applied to a clear, glass-like characteristic under microscopic examination.

Hypertension.   High blood pressure, when applied to heart function.

Hyperthyroidism.   Abnormal function of the thyroid gland characterized by excessive secretion of thyroid hormone.

Hypothalamus.   A part of the diencephalon concerned with important involuntary neural and neuroendocrine regulatory functions.

Hypertrophy.   Excessive growth.

Hypothyroidism.   A condition caused by the abnormally low production of thyroid hormone.

Identical (homozygous) twins.   Twins that develop from a single fertilized egg cell by its complete division or separation during mitosis (division).

Inspiration. The act of inhalation.

Involution. The return to a former, more primitive condition or previous form (e.g., the involution of the uterus after birth); also, a degenerative change.

Ischemic heart disease. A disease of the heart involving inadequate circulation of blood to the myocardium, usually as a result of coronary artery disease.

Ketone body. Product of fatty acid metabolism found in the blood and urine in abnormally high amounts in *diabetes mellitus* (especially *acetoacetic acid* and *beta-hydroxybutyric acid*), resulting in *metabolic acidosis* or *acid* condition of the blood and cells.

Kyphosis. An exaggerated, forward spinal curvature in the thoracic region.

Larynx. The cartilaginous voice box.

Lesion. Any injury or pathological change in a tissue that affects its structure or function.

LH. *See* Luteinizing hormone.

Libido. Conscious or unconscious sexual drive.

Life expectancy. The statistical prediction of how long an organism will live beyond a given initial age.

Lipase. A digestive enzyme that breaks down fats into simpler component fatty acids or smaller chains of fatty acids.

Lipid. A fat or fat-like substance.

Lipofuscin. Brown pigment granules representing lipid-containing residues of lysosomal digestion, usually occurring with increased incidence with advancing age in certain tissues.

Luteinizing hormone (LH). The hormone produced by the pituitary gland that stimulates the final ripening of the follicles of the ovaries, their rupture to release the ovum, and the conversion of the ruptured follicle into the corpus luteum.

Maturation. Ripening.

Medulla. The internal central part of a gland or organ.

Medulla oblongata. The expanded, bulb-like part of the spinal cord extending forward into the brain.

Melanocytes.   Cells producing the black melanin pigment.

Meninges.   Thin, protective sheet-like membranes that cover the brain and spinal cord (the pia mater, arachnoid, and dura mater).

Menopause.   The termination of the menstrual cycle and reproductive capacity in women; the climacteric.

Menstrual cycle.   The progression of uterine and ovarian changes and associated phenomena in women, usually occurring on a monthly basis.

Metabolism.   The sum total of the chemical changes occurring in various cells of the body involving both anabolism (build-up) and catabolism (breakdown) of organic compounds.

Microvilli.   Minute finger-like projections from the surface of certain epithelial cells of the intestinal lining.

Mitochondria.   Small granules or rod-shaped structures in the cytoplasm of cells involved in the generation of energy in their overall metabolism.

Motor nerve.   *See* Nerve, motor.

Muscular dystrophy.   A disease involving progressive muscle atrophy and accompanying weakness.

Muscle, skeletal (voluntary).   Muscle involved in movements of the limbs, head, and trunk; muscles under voluntary control.

Muscle, smooth (involuntary).   Muscle tissue of organs not under conscious control, such as of the bladder, stomach, and intestine.

Myasthenia gravis.   A chronic, progressive muscular weakness, beginning usually in the face or throat, unaccompanied by atrophy.

Nerve fibers.   Protoplasmic prolongations of the cell bodies of neurons (dendrites or axons).

Nerve, motor.   A nerve controlling muscles or glands.

Nerve, sensory.   A nerve transmitting impulses from a sense organ to the central nervous system (afferent nerve).

Nerve tracts.   Bundles or groups of nerve fibers within the central nervous system (the brain or spinal cord).

Neoplasm.   Any new growth of cells or tissues; a term customarily used to denote a cancer.

Neurohypophysis.   The posterior pituitary.

Neuron.   A nerve cell.

Olfactory bulb.   A mass of sensory cells in the upper nasal region concerned with the sense of smell.

Oocytes.   Immature ova.

Organ.   A part or member of an organism's body adapted for some particular function, usually consisting of a number of tissues (e.g., brain, kidney, liver).

Osmoreceptors.   Sensory cells that respond to changes in the osmotic pressure of the blood (probably located in the hypothalamus).

Osteoarthritis.   Inflammation of the articular extremities of bone resulting from structural changes in the cartilage and degeneration of the bones with osteophytic growths (bony outgrowths).

Osteomalacia.   A disease characterized by the gradual softening and bending of bones and usually accompanied by pain.

Osteoporosis.   A gradual resorption of bone such that the tissue becomes unusually porous and fragile.

Ovum (*pl.* ova).   The female gamete or germ cell (the mature egg).

Oxytocin.   A hormone produced by the neurohypophysis (posterior pituitary) whose principal action is on milk ejection in the lactating animal.

Paranoia.   A chronic mental disorder characterized by systematized delusions of persecution and self-importance.

Parathyroid glands.   Two pairs of endocrine glands lying on or embedded in the thyroid gland that produce hormones involved in calcium and phosphorus metabolism.

Parkinsonism.   A degenerative disease of the nervous system, characteristic of middle-aged and older persons, and characterized by rigidity, resting tremor, and fidgety or wasteful movements during walking or speaking.

Pathogeric.   Referring to any age-related disease state.

Pepsin.   A stomach enzyme that breaks down proteins into smaller components.

Periodontal.   Investing or around a tooth or teeth.

Peripheral resistance.   The resistance of the blood vessels (arteries and small arterioles) against which the heart pumps.

Peristalsis.   The rhythmic contractions of the muscular walls of the digestive system that move food along the system, help to break it down, and mix it with digestive secretions.

Pharynx.   A common structure below the mouth into which the Eustachian tubes of the ears and the nares empty and from which the esophagus and larynx lead posteriorly.

Pitch.   That property of a musical tone determined by the frequency of vibration of sound waves which strike the ear. The greater the frequency, the higher the pitch.

Pituitary.   An endocrine gland situated in the diencephalon region of the brain; it consists of an anterior lobe (the adenohypophysis) and a posterior lobe (the neurohypophysis).

Plaques, argyrophilic.   Flat, patch-like regions in tissues that take up silver-based stains in histological preparations.

Plaques, pigment.   Flat, patch-like regions in tissues that contain pigments like lipofuscin.

Plasma.   The liquid portion of the blood.

Pleiotrophic gene.   Any gene that involves the expression of more than one inheritable, visible characteristic (e.g., both skin and hair color).

Pleura.   The moist, membranous linings covering the lungs.

Pneumonia.   A disease of the lungs characterized by inflammation and excess fluid in the lung spaces, due either to viral or bacterial invasion or to chemical irritants.

Polymer.   A natural or synthetic chemical compound consisting of a series of repeating structural units or molecules.

Postmitotic.   A term applied to a state when cells are incapable of undergoing cell division.

Precursor.   A molecule that enters into some reaction to become something else.

Presbyopia.   Loss of the ability of the eye to accommodate to close vision which occurs in middle age.

Progesterone.   A steroid hormone produced by the placenta and corpus luteum that causes proliferative changes in the breasts and uterine endometrium.

Prolactin.   A gonadotrophic hormone produced by the adenohypophysis inducing milk secretion from the breasts which are primed by estrogen and progesterone; the lactogenic hormone.

Protein.   The basic component of living protoplasm that consists of nitrogenous compounds made up of many amino acids.

Protoplasm.   The contents of a cell consisting of the cytoplasm and nucleus, but excluding vacuoles, mitochondria, lysosomes, etc.

Ptyalin (salivary amylase).   An enzyme found in saliva that is responsible for digesting starch in the mouth.

Pulmonary.   Pertaining to the lungs.

Pulmonary emboli.   Blood clots blocking the tiny blood vessels of the lungs.

Pulse rate.   The rate of rhythmical pulsations of the arteries that reflects the heart rate.

Pyelonephritis.   A serious inflammation of the kidneys.

Pyridoxine (vitamin B6).   A vitamin associated with the utilization of unsaturated fatty acids.

Quinone.   A complex organic compound with a structure such as to serve chiefly as an oxidizing agent.

Radiation, ionizing.   High-level energy, such as that from certain radioactive atoms or X-rays, capable of the production of charged particles (ions) in the cells or tissues that it penetrates.

Reflex.   A predictable response to a given stimulus by a sensory nerve cell or cells.

Renal plasma flow.   The amount of plasma flowing into the parts of the kidney that have a function in the production of urine (measured using the chemicals diodrast or para-aminohippuric acid as a marker substance).

Respiratory minute volume.   The amount of air moved into and out of the respiratory passages each minute.

Ribosome.   Small discrete cell particles consisting of ribonucleic acid and occuring in the cytoplasm. They are involved in protein synthesis.

Saturated fats.   Fats of which the carbon atoms all contain the maximum number of hydrogen atoms.

Sclerosis.   Hardening.

Secretion.　The release of biologically active substances from glands or the matter secreted.

Seminal fluid.　The secretion from the male sex organs and accessory glands that contains spermatozoa and associated substances.

Seminiferous tubules.　Tubes in the testes through which newly produced sperm move outward.

Senescence.　The degenerative phase of the aging process.

Senile dementia.　Severe mental deterioration in old age, associated with brain atrophy and loss of memory, learning ability, and adaptability.

Sensory nerve.　*See* Nerve, sensory.

Septum.　A partition or wall.

Sequela.　An adverse or morbid condition left as a result of a disease.

Somatic cells.　All the cells of the body other than the germ cells.

Spermatozoa.　The male germ cells; also called sperm.

Sphincter.　A circular muscle surrounding and capable of closing an opening (e.g., the sphincter of the iris or of the pyloric region of the stomach).

Stereotype.　A fixed or general notion or image, undistinguished by individuality.

Steroids.　Compounds containing mainly carbon and hydrogen with most carbon atoms arranged in adjoining rings. Steroids include cholesterol, the sex hormones, and hormones of the adrenal cortex.

Stroke.　Blockage or breakage of a blood vessel accompanied by brain cell damage and usually followed by neurological deficits of some kind.

Syphilis.　A chronic, specific, contagious venereal disease caused by the microorganism *Treponema pallidum*.

Systole.　The contraction phase of the cardiac cycle.

Systolic pressure.　The arterial blood pressure during active contraction (systole) of the ventricles of the heart.

Tachycardia.　Rapid heartbeat due either to disease or to physiological stress (such as exercise).

Taste bud.　An organ in the mouth responsible for the sense of taste.

Testosterone.   The most important male sex hormone that is chiefly responsible for the development of the secondary male sex characteristics (deep voice, hairy body, and beard).

Threshold.   The minimal level of stimulation necessary to evoke a particular physiological response.

Thrombus.   A blood clot formed within the circulatory system (e.g., coronary thrombus).

Thyroid gland.   A bilobed, shield-shaped endocrine gland that produces thyroxine. It is located in the neck attached to the trachea just below the larynx.

Thyroid-releasing factor (TRF).   The hypothalamic hormone responsible for stimulation of TSH production by the pituitary gland.

Thyroid-stimulating hormone (TSH).   A hormone produced by the anterior lobe of the pituitary gland that stimulates the thyroid gland to produce thyroxine.

Thyroxine.   The hormone produced by the thyroid gland that is responsible for tissue metabolism.

Tidal volume.   The amount of air inhaled or exhaled during a single cycle of quiet respiration.

Tinnitus.   A purely subjective whistling, ringing or other sensation of noise in the ear.

Tissue, connective.   A tissue that supports or binds together other types of tissues. In most of the body, it forms the framework for the body organs.

Touch corpuscle.   Any one of a number of sensory receptors responsible for the sense of touch.

Trace elements.   Elements present in minute amounts in the diet and in the body (iron, zinc, copper, manganese, etc.). A number of these are vital for the production of important body products such as thyroxine, insulin, and hemoglobin.

Trachea.   The windpipe that leads from the pharynx to the bronchi.

Transcription (genetic).   The transfer of genetic information from the DNA in the nucleus to RNA, the substance ultimately responsible for protein synthesis in the cytoplasm.

Translation (genetic).   The synthesis of amino acid chains and proteins by messenger RNA carrying the specific genetic information for such syntheses.

Trophic.   Pertaining to nutrition; commonly applied to hormones inducing the production of other hormones.

TRF.   *See* Thyroid-releasing factor.

Trypsin.   An enzyme secreted by the pancreas into the small intestine that digests protein.

TSH.   *See* Thyroid-stimulating hormone.

Tuberculosis.   An infectious disease caused by the tubercle bacillus that most commonly occurs in the lungs and less frequently in bone, lymph glands, intestines, kidneys, or skin.

Tumor.   An abnormal mass of tissue arising without apparent cause and unrestricted in growth.

Unsaturated fats.   Lipid or fatty compounds containing one or more *double bonds,* a structure rendering them more readily soluble in fat solvents and having lower melting points than saturated fats; usually liquid at room temperatures (e.g., oleic and linoleic acids). When saturated by catalytic addition of hydrogen atoms, these become solidified and less soluble in fat solvents.

Urethra.   The tube leading out of the bladder through which urine is passed out of the body.

Vacuole.   A small cavity in the protoplasm of a living cell containing fluid.

Vagina.   The passageway from the uterus to the outside of the body.

Vascular.   Of or pertaining to a vessel (tube) through which a fluid (blood) flows.

Vasodilation.   The enlarging of the openings of blood vessels (especially arteries).

Vasopressin.   A hormone secreted by the posterior pituitary (neurohypophysis) that inhibits the production of urine.

Ventricle.   A thick-walled chamber of the heart that receives blood from the atria and pumps it into a large artery (the pulmonary artery or aorta).

Villi.   Finger-like processes extending from the inner surface of the small intestine that are responsible for absorption of digestion products into the bloodstream.

Virilism.   An abnormality in women marked by the presence of secondary sexual characteristics of the male (e.g., excessive amounts of hair, deep voice, skeletal form, etc.).

Vital capacity.   The amount of air that can be expired by the most forcible expiration following a maximal inspiration.

Vitamin.   An organic compound that, in minute amounts, is essential for normal metabolic functioning of the body.

Void.   To excrete, as in urinating or defecating.

Vulva.   The external female genital structures.

General References

Agate, J. 1963. The practice of geriatrics. Charles C. Thomas, Springfield, Ill. 490 pp.

Andrew, W. 1971. The anatomy of aging in man and animals. Grune and Stratton, New York. 259 pp.

Bellak, L. 1975. The best years of your life. Atheneum, New York. 297 pp.

Binstock, R. H., and E. Shanas, eds. 1977. Handbook of aging and the social sciences. Van Nostrand Reinhold, New York. 684 pp.

Birren, J. E., and K. W. Schaie, eds. 1977. Handbook of the psychology of aging. Van Nostrand Reinhold, New York. 700 pp.

Brocklehurst, J. C., ed. 1973. Textbook of geriatric medicine and gerontology. Churchill Livingstone, Edinburgh. 760 pp.

Butler, R. N. 1975. Why survive? Being old in America. Harper & Row, New York. 496 pp.

Comfort, A. 1964. Aging: The biology of senescence. Holt, Reinhart and Winston, New York. 365 pp.

Finch, C. E., and L. Hayflick, eds. 1977. Handbook of the biology of aging. Van Nostrand Reinhold, New York. 771 pp.

Freeman, J. T., ed. 1965. Clinical features of the older patient. Charles C. Thomas, Springfield, Ill. 491 pp.

Goldman, R., M. Rockstein, and M. Sussman, eds. 1975. The physiology and pathology of human aging. Academic Press, New York. 232 pp.

Guyton, A. C. 1976. Textbook of medical physiology. W. B. Saunders, Philadelphia. 1194 pp.

Korenchevsky, V. 1961. Physiological and pathological aging. S. Karger, Basel. 514 pp.

Kormondy, E. J., T. F. Sherman, F. B. Salisbury, N. T. Spratt, Jr., and G. McCain. 1977. Biology. Wadsworth, Belmont, Ca. 482 pp.

Lansing, A. I., ed. 1952. Cowdry's problems of aging. Williams & Wilkins, Baltimore. 1061 pp.

Metropolitan Life Insurance Company. *Statistical Bulletin(s)*.

Ostfeld, A. M., and D. C. Gibson. 1972. Epidemiology of aging. U.S. Dept. of Health, Education and Welfare, Bethesda, Md. 286 pp.

Timiras, P. S. 1972. Developmental physiology and aging. Macmillan, New York. 692 pp.

Working with older people. 1972. I. The practitioner and the elderly. U.S. Dept. of Health, Education and Welfare HSM 72–6005. Rockville, Md. 54 pp.

Working with older people. 1974. II. Biological, psychological and sociological aspects of aging. U.S. Dept. of Health, Education and Welfare HSM 72–6006. Rockville, Md. 51 pp.

Working with older people. 1974. III. The aging person: Needs and services. U.S. Dept. of Health, Education and Welfare HSM 72–6007. Rockville, Md. 90 pp.

Working with older people. 1971. IV. Clinical aspects of aging. U.S. Dept. of Health, Education and Welfare 1459IV. Rockville, Md. 388 pp.

Index

54 W 0560
ISBN 0-534-00687-6